SIGOURNEY WEAVER

SIGOURNEY WEAVER

T. D. Maguffee

ST. MARTIN'S PRESS
NEW YORK

Library of Congress Cataloging-in-Publication Data

Maguffee, T. D.
        Sigourney Weaver / T.D. Maguffee.
                p.   cm.
        "A Thomas Dunne book."
        ISBN 0-312-02980-2
        1. Weaver, Sigourney.   2. Motion picture actors and
actresses—United States—Biography.   I. Title.
        PN2287.W4548.M34 1989
        791.43′028′0924—dc 19
        [B]   89-4068
                                                              CIP

A 2M Communications Ltd. Production.

First U.S. Edition
10 9 8 7 6 5 4 3 2 1

To Nancy—whose energy, courage, and positive spirit will live in my heart and actions forever.

1

She is Ripley, and we are with her as she battles a fourteen-foot high monster, one that could only live in the outermost regions of unexplored space or the innermost regions of our imaginations. It is *High Noon, Gunfight at the OK Coral*, and *Shane* relived, yet this time the action does not center on one man against one man, but on one woman against a female of another life form. It is classic motion picture art, but it is uniquely different, too.

Ripley is shown fighting with all the skills and courage she possesses for things that are obvious to all of us as good. For as long as there have been cameras and film, this is what the hero is supposed to do. And just like almost all of the great cinematic heroes of the past, she hadn't asked to save the world, she hadn't asked to be the one needed by the world, but by a stroke of fate and timing it fell upon her to carry the torch for all of us, and that fact makes her one of us, a hero all of us hope we could be, and one we desperately want to see beating the odds and winning the climactic victory.

Now, of course, Sigourney Weaver is the only one any of us can imagine, outside of ourselves, possibly playing the part of Ripley . . . and play her she did. She was so good that when the nominations for the Academy Awards for the films of 1986 were announced, something unheard of happened. A woman starring in a science fiction/fantasy role claimed one of the five spots reserved for best performance by a leading actress. Just like Ripley, Sigourney Weaver had beaten the odds. Yet in retrospect, who among us would have originally cast her in that role? In real life she doesn't seem the Rambo-of-outer-space type.

It was seven years between the time that she first starred as Ripley in *Alien* and then repeated the same role in *Aliens*. In that time, her life changed and we grew to know her as a star. Yet in a world priding itself on delivering every bit of insignificant information that could possibly exist on every famous and pseudo-famous person who is now living, she has remained out of the headlines, off the interview shows, and has usually escaped the tabloids. She is almost as big a mystery now as she was when she made her debut.

Who is Sigourney Weaver? What is she really like? Where does she come from? Answering these questions is as difficult as catching a butterfly. For one thing, it is hard to pin her down. She is both honest and vague at the same time. She is both brilliant and often illogical. She is the modern American woman who, somehow, still conjures up visions of actresses from the golden age of Hollywood. She is very much one of a kind, and yet to fully describe her acting (as well as her life) one must use comparisons of people and events that immediately lump her with someone from another time and place.

While it is true that like all great actresses she brings a bit of herself to each of her roles, she is not Ripley nor is she Jill Bryant from *Year of Living Dangerously,* or really any of a dozen other characters she has portrayed in her career. She shows the unique ability to step into a character and then walk away from it. It was often said of the late Cary Grant that he always played Cary Grant. Sigourney Weaver doesn't play herself; she becomes a role and then, when she completes it, leaves it behind. So, if you are looking for the real Cary Grant, go to see a few of his movies. But if you want to begin to understand something about Sigourney Weaver, watching her films will reveal little of her past, her present, or her future, but it will reveal what most of the world already knows: She is one great actress.

In the movie *Alien* we discovered her, but we never learned all that much about her character, and little was offered in the way of probing dialogue or background information. We were forced to accept Ripley just as she was. Even when the movie was over and we left our seats to go home, we wondered little about either Ripley or Sigourney Weaver, and we spoke even less of them. We were just glad that Ripley had made it out alive. Still, even though the film made $30 million and even though we loved it for what it was, it was not "art." It wasn't a movie we were going to talk about in terms other than a big "boo!" Orson Wells was still able to retain ownership rights to Hollywood's best feature.

So, when the sequel came into our theaters, when we were given an opportunity to once again be treated to a few more big boos, we expected little more than the original. And while we may have looked forward to some great special effects and more gross-out slime scenes, we didn't expect anything in the way of character development or expansive roles. We were glad that Sigourney Weaver was back as Ripley, but until the moment when we saw her repeating the role, most of us figured that an actress like Sybil Danning, "Queen of the Adventure Flicks," could have played the part, too. We were all proven wrong.

If *Alien* gave Sigourney her first break, *Aliens* proved that she deserved recognition as a star. For despite the great writing, pacing, and wonderful special effects of the latter film, her performance was responsible for raising it from a B picture to one of the best movies in any category released in 1986.

In *Aliens,* Sigourney brought the two-dimensional Ripley alive. She brought fabric, emotion, and strength to a role that few other actresses would have considered important. Just as generations of film buffs and fans walked down the deserted streets of a western town with Gary Cooper in *High Noon,* generations will walk step by step through the *Aliens'* space station with Ms. Weaver. It is a rare actor or actress who becomes immersed in a part so deeply that each person who watches becomes that part, too. Sigourney Weaver made us care deeply about Ripley . . . we wanted her to be real and alive, on our side. And winning.

How did she do it? What in her background allowed her to bring so much to a role seemingly meant for so little? What rare qualities make her so very special in a business where real stardom is often decided more by whim and luck than by true talent?

Just as Ripley became more than we expected, Sigourney and her background offered each of us much more than we could ever guess. This is not a woman of simple background and big dreams. This is not the story of a small-town girl who used all her grit to work her way up and become a star.

Far from it. This is the story of a family whose privileged lifestyle, energy, and creativity were legendary. It is the story of a child conceived in a world of glitz and glitter, and brought up in a family that knew few boundaries, surrounded as it was by position and money and power.

If all of this sounds like a formula for a romance novel, well, it is one that has probably been used over and over again. But this story is real, and the seeds of Sigourney's depth and passion, probably the two most important and unique qualities of her life, go back for at least two generations. It is there, before the turn of century in a wide-open Los Angeles, over eighty years ago and thousands of miles from the soundstages in London where *Aliens* was filmed, that her story really begins.

2

Good genes. Few people are blessed with them on even one side of the family tree, but Sigourney Weaver has more than her share. In fact, the roots of her creativity, boundless energy, and a lust for life go down deep. For the actress the formula of success can be traced and observed in the actions and lives of not only her parents, but a particular set of grandparents, too.

Sylvester Weaver Sr., Sigourney's paternal grandfather, was an easterner who followed Horace Greeley's call and moved west, becoming one of southern California's most stable and educated early settlers. He wasn't after gold in the hills; far from it. His vision was to build something much more elaborate and lasting.

Sylvester Weaver was nothing if not an astute businessman. Soon after hitting the city of angels he recognized an area of trade that he felt was going to grow in a big way. Nothing ever stopped Sylvester Weaver for very long and few things ever slowed him down, so, reacting to his vision, he plunged into the construction game, eventually becoming one of the area's leading roofing manufacturers. He was so good and developed his business so well that he soon became one of the region's first non-gold mining self-made millionaires.

Success came to Sylvester Weaver Sr. because he was more than just a good businessman. He was a promoter and he was an ideas person. He was someone who could have been successful in any era or place, because he could seemingly forecast the future and therefore get the jump on tomorrow. He combined all of this with a special charm, so he was also well-respected and liked. There is little doubt that his vision and hard work changed his adopted home state a great deal. He was at the heart of the creation and growth of a whole new way of life. A part of the vision and lust for life that we think of as special to California and Californians may have had some beginnings, or at least some of the special fire, in Sylvester Weaver's mind and heart.

Sigourney's grandmother was a perfect match for the mover and shaker of her businessman husband. He may have left his mark on a host of buildings, and he may have been a king on Main Street, but she didn't have to stand in the background and occasionally be introduced as Mrs. Weaver. She made a spotlight all for herself.

She was born in Ohio, and long before she married, long before she had given birth to four children, she was viewed as a most talented and gifted person. In a world where proper women were background creatures, considered more suitable as decorations, she charged in and won respect for her beauty and her brains. She was ahead of her time, and perhaps it was this quality that first perked the farsighted Sylvester Weaver to notice her.

Her interests were not limited to but certainly centered around the art forms. She loved to read, and she loved to share what she had learned through her reading with others. When she wasn't reading, she was writing poetry, composing operas, or playing various musical instruments. While her husband may have supplied southern California with building materials, she helped to build an appreciation for culture in the region. She was lady who never stopped expanding her world or her mind. It certainly didn't hurt that her husband was able to purchase anything needed for this quest. Certainly his money proved a ransom to rescue her from the hard life of being a wife and mother in the early part of this century.

Mr. and Mrs. Weaver lived in a world of privilege. Certainly they earned it. And this world (as well as their money) allowed them to grace not only themselves but their children with special opportunities that hardly any children of the west had ever experienced. Their four children, two boys and two girls, received the best opportunities for education and cultural growth both at home and in school. They never lacked for anything material, and had a real security that few children, even those born today, ever know. There was plenty of food, clothes, trips, and a hearty helping of fun, too.

It was into this ideal world, in 1908, that Sylvester Weaver Jr. was born. And long before he would be known as Sigourney Weaver's father, and long after he was known as Sylvester's son, he would become one of the nation's most influential leaders in a fledgling industry. An industry that he molded and shaped in a way few men have.

It was obvious from his toddler years that Sylvester Jr., nicknamed Pat, was gifted in many of the same artistic areas as his mother. But it was also obvious that he had his father's knack for business. By the time he was in grammar school he had published his own newspaper, *The Eagle;* had mastered the game of chess; had read Gibbon's *Decline and Fall of the Roman Empire;* and had learned the roofing business from the ground up. He would later say, "I knew the ins and outs of business before I knew about girls." He was a small sponge soaking up everything. Yet there was more to him than just books and studies. He had his father's boundless energy, too.

Pat was a good baseball player, a winner at tennis, and by the time he hit his early teens he had taken an old Ford Motel T, cut it down, customized it, and was sporting about in the California sunshine in a hot rod long before the term was invented. He was an expert at the Charleston and fox trot, and he graduated from Los Angeles High at the top of his class. In his spare hours, he was one of the city's best-known men-about-town.

In the late 1920s, while still in his late teens, Pat Weaver began to make his mark on the Los Angeles social scene. By now he was six feet four inches in height and his imposing frame seemed a perfect hanger for dinner jackets and formal clothes. He began to make all the town's big parties with the likes of Joan Crawford and Carole Lombard on his arm. He was "the" date for any debutante, and he must have enjoyed playing the field. With an everpresent smile on his face, he owned every situation he encountered and was capable of charming almost any person he met. He could have been the prototype hero for any novel, and lived the life of a movie star. Who knows what might have become of this once serious student, now a fledgling playboy, if he hadn't headed east for Dartmouth.

At the Ivy League institution, books once again became Pat Weaver's love. He didn't quit girls and parties, but he also didn't let them control the increasingly important part of his life. Like his mother, he had a lust for knowledge and growth, and he didn't want to be confined to the world he was born into. He wanted to make a new one of his own. Therefore, he studied. During his college years, he made Phi Beta Kappa, majored in philosophy, and constantly amazed both professors and students alike with his wit, insight, and ability to convert learning into action. He was one of a kind and he left a lasting impression on everyone who came in contact with him.

After school, and during the entire year of 1930, Weaver trekked around Europe and the Middle East. Money was not a problem for this millionaire's son, so he enjoyed taking in the ruins of which he had read so much. He lived a life of adventure and romance. While studying the past, he began to get a vision of the future. Of course, he also enjoyed the Old World nightlife as well as the charms of its women.

Returning to the States in the midst of the Depression in 1931, tiring of wandering and spinning his wheels, Weaver tried his hand at a number of businesses. He finally landed in radio. It was a wonderful world for him. It was to Pat what the building trade had been in southern California to his father—a chance to make his mark in an area that was just taking off. It was a place to let his mind run wild, where he wouldn't have to hear "It couldn't be done" because there were so few things that had been tried. He worked night and day, made jumps from station to station, and constantly became better at what he was doing. Rarely had radio ever been this much fun.

He first tasted real success in San Francisco in the midthirties, but by late 1935 he had discovered that, on the airwaves, the real money and power were on the East Coast. So he headed back. There was a host of folks in California who believed that he would not only find success there, but would soon be running the whole show, too.

Mort Werner, later an NBC producer, knew Weaver during his initial days in radio. He was one of many who thought the boy wonder was from a different planet. Werner once said of Weaver, "He's the only man that I know who can reminisce about the future." Such was the man's talent and insight.

During this phase of his career, Weaver

could certainly look into the future. He found the stars, wrote and produced their shows, and always seemed to be just one gimmick ahead of the competition. He dreamed of the way things should be and then did them. He was responsible for signing such stars as Fred Allen and Jack Benny, and he helped to make NBC a real leader and force in the industry. It seemed as if he had nowhere to go but right up the corporate ladder to the top.

Still, he was bored easily once he had accomplished something. So, feeling that he had few avenues of imagination left at NBC, he left radio in 1938 and jumped into the advertising game. Quickly his ideas and imagination made him a success in that field, but it didn't challenge him enough either. So he moved into a $5,000-a-year job with another monied Dartmouth classmate named Nelson Rockefeller. Together they beamed American propaganda to Latin America via the radio. Propaganda had never been so entertaining or effective. It was during this period of unique service, a stint where Weaver again created most of his own rules and blazed his own trails, that his life would change.

He had been a wanderer. He had taken life by storm, running through every rainstorm, challenging every mountain, visiting venues that interested him only long enough to discover that there was another place he hadn't been and taking off for it again. But something during another routine stop would change him. In a way it would limit him, but it would also force him to channel his energy in a singular direction for a while. He would gain a bit of stability and responsibility, and the only cost would be his single, playboy status. Pat Weaver finally found someone to share his life (and some of his adventures) with him, someone who came up to his standards in every way. Someone whose star shone more brightly than all the debutantes and Hollywood actresses he'd met.

Her name was Elizabeth Inglis. British and a fine stage actress, she was also a dark-haired beauty with a keen intelligence. She had worked for masters of creativity such as Alfred Hitchcock, and a host of men had attempted to catch her with their good looks, presents, and charms, but it was Pat Weaver who caught her attention and then won her love. She was so charmed by him that she gave up her career and homeland to marry him. Now well into his thirties, Pat Weaver had finally made the last step toward growing up.

World War II interrupted the Weavers' first year of bliss. Pat entered the Navy and became a PC boat skipper. Lieutenant Weaver took to the salt air as well as he had taken to radio. He was a favorite with his crew and his fellow officers, although also a breed apart. He rarely put on a full uniform, preferring to sit on the deck soaking up the sun's rays. He knew that war was a life-or-death business, but he knew that fun was important, too. No war would get in the way of his laughter or wit.

He spent his spare time writing, working on an unpublished novel called *Tomorrow* as well as planning things to do in both radio and advertising, but mainly he just looked forward to going back to New York. Weaver knew that his mark on history had not yet been made, and he knew that it wouldn't be made in the Navy. Pat Weaver wanted to change the world, and he couldn't wait to find a way to do it.

After the war and after the birth of a son, Trajan, named after Pat's favorite Roman general, Weaver returned to New York and the American Tobacco Company. He was in charge of advertising. Still, it was old hat to the farsighted Weaver, and he yearned to be challenged by something new, something exciting. He felt that his creativity, and therefore his time, was being wasted. He had far too much energy just to do things that he knew "ordinary men with ordinary dreams" could do.

When, in 1947, he was offered a job with the NBC television network, he took it immediately. Initially he was put in charge of the development of color broadcast, but he was moved to programming soon thereafter. NBC needed more than color to keep from being buried by CBS. At the time NBC was a network without any clear-cut vision, and in a medium depending on loyal viewers, that was disastrous. They needed a change—a big change.

Meanwhile, Weaver was in heaven, working in a field that was completely new. He could help create rules, and he wouldn't be limited by years of regression thinking. Here was a place where he could build. His excitement was obvious in every step he took and everything he said. While a good portion of the country and so-called experts were laughing at television as something that would never really work, Weaver, recognizing its real future and its real uses, saw it as the most important invention of the modern era. He knew that America, and the world, needed this little box and the pictures and messages it could send out.

NBC, struggling in the new medium, needed men like Pat Weaver, too. They were pouring money into something that was so far returning nothing. Many of the executives wondered if it just wouldn't be better to dump what they were working on and go back to radio. After all, they had only twenty-five affiliated stations and thirty-seven hours of programming per week. Yet this was just the idea vacuum Weaver had needed, and he began to brainstorm, envisioning things no one else had ever seen. It was hard to believe they could work. Given time, he would convince everyone.

In one of their better decisions at the time, NBC moved Weaver to the top of the programming ladder. The network was almost in a panic. Week in and week out CBS was beating them handily in the ratings, and everything they had tried seemed to bomb.

Just like the marines battling the space monsters in *Aliens,* Weaver walked in and took over a situation that had seemed totally lost. It was right where he wanted to be.

Weaver initially shocked staff members at meetings by proposing that NBC offer a series of one-hour "spectaculars." These would consist of an hour of special programming where high-powered, famous stars—stars like Frank Sinatra—would have a chance to entertain an audience from coast to coast in a one-time-only event. Everyone said it wouldn't work; the critics laughed. But almost forty years later, television viewers everywhere look forward to these special events, and networks use them during the "sweep" periods in order to pull big ratings.

Weaver also proposed a new morning show. He wanted it to be live, featuring interviews and a magazine-style format, with news, weather, and real people. He actually had to convince NBC that people would turn on their sets in the morning to watch what was offered. Before this move, networks had considered the morning to be dead time and completely unprofitable. Weaver called his new show *Today.* Today, thirty-five years af-

SIGOURNEY WEAVER • 23

ter it kicked off on NBC with a chimpanzee as a cohost and Dave Garroway as its anchor, the show is still a winner.

There in a set in Radio City, where visitors could look through the plate-glass windows to see Dave Garroway at work every morning on *Today*, Weaver watched the world become believers in his morning concept. It must have pleased him immensely, although before long he was back at work dictating more, necessary changes at the network. His rambling memos became the Biblical notes of an industry. Not only did NBC anxiously await what he said in these daily bulletins, but the press published them and the other networks studied and debated them for hours.

His next successful creation was a late night show called *Tonight*. Steve Allen was the original host. He gave way to Jack Parr who gave way to Johnny Carson, but it took Pat Weaver to give birth to it. Once again, on that first night, not many besides its creator believed that America would buy it. Why would people stay up until all hours of the night just to watch a bunch of people telling jokes and stories? Weaver knew why, and he was proven right again.

Under Weaver, NBC took off. It was no longer lost in a mass of poor programming and indecision. It was alive with new ideas; stars like Bob Hope, Dave Garroway, Dinah Shore, Steve Allen, and a growing host of others. It was the place where creative people wanted to be, and it was demonstrating techniques and formats that the whole world would copy. And Weaver was at the heart of every decision. Like a prophet he was followed everywhere he went.

He had taken a skeleton and fleshed it out. He had taken an expensive novelty and made it an institution. He had made television a must for everyone, not just in the evenings, but around the clock. He had seen more and then delivered more than anyone could have expected.

And it was into this fast-paced, creative, always alive and changing world that a daughter was born. She was christened Susan. Just like everything else Pat Weaver had helped create, she would be unique and a winner.

3

Susan Weaver was born on October 8, 1949 into anything but an ordinary world. With father Pat now whirling around making decisions affecting the entire evolution of television; with a literal who's who of New York society and the entertainment industry constantly showing up at the Weaver apartment to bounce her on a famous knee while visiting with her father; with nannies, maids, and chauffeurs at beck and call; and with formal dinners and wonderfully orchestrated vacations; her life was, to say the least, privileged.

She was a princess born into a family where her father was the king of network television. In 1949, network (or what little there was of it) was the *only* kind of television.

But did being born into a show business circus really mark Susan for a career in the arts? She would later remark, "In my family, show business was part of our world. I don't think I got a chance to see what something else would be like. I didn't mean to go into show business, but I think I naturally gravitated toward it." How could she help but desire a life that seemed so normal for her, and a life that offered her so many wonderful experiences? Having everything was fun. Being at the center of an exciting life, with a whirlwind of different and exciting people, makes a mark even on the smallest of children.

For the first seven years of her life, from 1949 to 1956, Susan's father headed the programming department at NBC. Because of this, her world was filled with family friends who naturally represented the powerful and best-known products of the new world of television. Entertainers were not merely visions on a small screen to her; they were a part of her everyday life.

There were a number of reasons why so

many movers and shakers found their way to the Weaver household. Pat did a great deal of his best thinking at home. A great number of his famous and lengthy staff memorandums were written during his off-hours. He never really stopped working. His mind was always reeling, filling up countless reams of paper with new ideas to make television better.

His working at home led to great numbers of people coming to him to discuss their ideas or how they might fit into his plans. Because Pat Weaver was committed to doing different things and forging new inroads in television programming, exciting and enthusiastic people were drawn to him. He offered them opportunities they may not have been able to find at the more conservative CBS.

Finally, even while away from work, the Weavers were people who enjoyed socializing. Because they had both been bred on the best in literature and the arts, the guests who often spent hours at their home were some of the classiest and most talented people in New York. Any child with average intelligence was going to absorb some of this atmosphere. Susan was far above the average, and she absorbed a great deal.

Her father and mother were not the only

Weaver family members involved in entertainment. The common man or woman on the street probably knew Susan's uncle better than the head of NBC. Doodles Weaver, often called by family members the most intelligent Weaver, made his living as a comic with the Spike Jones Band. He was constantly making little Susan and her older brother Trajan laugh. The American public loved his antics, and though he wasn't involved in the serious science of making the decisions as to what the country would be seeing every night on the tube, his kind of work was probably a bit more fascinating to Susan, too. He was a real showman.

But while Doodles was a clown and showman, Pat's manner could instill awe in a great number of people. He believed in himself, and this belief was transmitted to those he contacted. When introducing the *Today Show* he very matter-of-factly proclaimed, "This program is a milestone in the social history of this country." Here was a man who didn't lack confidence in his own ideas. His children developed immense security despite their constantly changing world, and certainly Pat Weaver's healthy self-confidence was a major reason for the family's overall stability—

an unusual stability in the face of show business chaos.

Early in Susan's life, Dave Garroway, the first host of the *Today Show,* was a regular visitor. *Today* was, and is, Pat Weaver's biggest programming success. But there was a parade of other important names in the Weaver home, too. Art Linkletter was a common sight around the household. On Christmas when Susan came down with the chicken pox, Art came by to see her. As she recalled, "No child enjoys being ill at Christmas time! But he [Linkletter] managed to cheer me up!" In fact, few children received housecalls from the host of *Houseparty* at any time of the year.

Milton Berle was another person who rang the Weaver doorbell a few times. And while Uncle Miltie may have been the top draw on prime-time television in the early fifties with his *Texaco Star Theater,* to the Weavers he was just another regular guest.

In a way Susan's home was a home without any real star egos, because almost everyone who came by was a star. There was no pulling of rank or social standing, and money meant little. This was a home of power and privilege, and the power belonged to the network head. Name value was not nearly as important as the impression of the individual. Certainly Steve Allen and Jessica Tandy made their marks, as did a host of other personalities of the day, but no one made a more lasting impression on Susan Weaver than J. Fred Muggs.

In the midfifties, Muggs became a household name and a beloved television personality as the chimpanzee weatherman on the original *Today Show.* America knew him as a funny and intelligent comedian, a genuinely nice animal. He and Dave Garroway seemed to work well together, and the chimp was often perceived as harmless and playful. The impression he left at the Weaver household was quite different.

"He was a vicious little beast," Susan remembered of her first alien encounter. "He tried to rip my dress off!" The move cost Muggs his visiting rights in the Weaver home, but it didn't keep him off the air. He remained a star, with a star's touchy personality, for some years to come. While he didn't make any points with Susan Weaver, the little ape did help to put *Today* on the map for NBC, consolidate Pat's power and prestige, and make a small fortune for the network.

Of course, even if J. Fred had made a good impression, finding the Weaver home for a return visit might have been a challenge. In Susan's first ten years of life the family moved no less than *thirty* times. They lived mostly in New York's East Fifties, but the vagabond spirit of Pat Weaver made sure they didn't live in any one place very long. He seemed to like to move as much as he did fiddling with the prime-time schedules.

Jokes about this lifestyle were often repeated at NBC. The one retold the most intimated that the Weavers moved whenever their present house needed cleaning. The real truth seemed to be found in Pat's love of the ocean. He would move whenever he found a room with a better view of the rivers surrounding Manhattan. He was also the kind of person who didn't want to be trapped by old ideas or rules, and constantly having a new horizon to look at may have helped him feel like he was improving his work as well as eliminating the boredom that still seemed to overtake him quite easily.

Throughout the late forties and fifties, the Weavers were an important part of the New York social set, and parties and openings kept them on the move. When they were at home, the constant storm of business and company kept them busy either working or entertaining. Therefore, the children were raised as much by hired help as by their parents. Still, because of the love and interest their parents did show when they were with them and, once again, because of the self-confidence that they recognized in their parents' actions, Susan and Trajan seemed to grow up very well-adjusted.

The fact that they were rich—and the fact that this wealth was not "new" wealth—gave even the very young Susan opportunities for growth and unique experiences. She not only met famous people regularly, but she learned manners, breeding, and culture. She wasn't as much a little girl as a little lady.

Culture was stressed in the Weaver household. Plays, literature, and classical music were immensely important to both parents. Because Susan's mother had once been a classically trained British stage actress, her love of the theater had not diminished after she had given up her career to marry Pat. She made sure her children were exposed early and often to the art she loved.

Pat took it a step further. He had a very

high view of what television should be and what it should do. In 1952 he told his staff, "The next decade depends more on us than anyone else, barring war." He felt a real pressure to uplift what Americans saw on television and he became almost obsessed with not only instilling in his children a love for all kinds of classics, but with finding a way to deliver this same kind of entertainment and culture to the American public.

In his children he found a willing audience, but the Americans who viewed the shows he placed on the air were a different matter. It seems they preferred to turn to the mindless fluff they could find on another channel. They didn't want to be educated; they wanted to be entertained. Ultimately, what made them feel good was different than what Pat Weaver and NBC were trying to force them to accept. In the long run, his numerous programming successes would not make up for his long and almost fruitless attempts at raising the cultural standards for the general public, who still preferred a good old shoot-'em-up western. It may have been his love and belief in the arts that would cause his eventual downfall.

Still, Pat's reign at NBC, even though ultimately not as successful toward the end as it had been early on, would continue for a while longer, and during this time Susan would be able to enjoy the wonders this powerful position opened to her more and more. She and Trajan spent hours backstage at Radio City Music Hall. To this day she recalled this one opportunity with as much if not more joy than any other when speaking of her childhood. Here was a place filled with excitement and fantasy. It was not unlike the world's largest playhouse, and it had a wide array of adventures for any imaginative child. Susan spent hours running around, discovering new sets, new nooks and crannies, and new ways to create fun. It was the ultimate dollhouse for any child, and she felt as if she owned it. As long as Pat remained in control of the network, in a way she did, too.

In addition to Radio City there were other television studios and tapings as well as the opportunity of being on the inside of the *Today Show* set, where thousands of New Yorkers stopped to look in through picture windows at the show while it was being beamed across the country. Life for Susan was one filled with the constantly changing marvels of television. She lived, in a sense, as the ultimate child raised by the tube, and unlike other children of the same generation, she got hers from the inside out rather than the outside in.

Not even Sigourney can say if her love of the arts began with the fun of those days or through the experiences she had from being around the movers and shakers of television, but they had to make an enormous impact. Another impact must have been made by the very environment that Pat Weaver had created in the countless homes where his family lived.

In every room there were televisions and radios. Not just one or two, but dozens. They were constantly on, constantly playing, always tuned to different stations and filling the air with a multitude of entertainment. Pat Weaver didn't want to miss anything, to stay far ahead of the rest of the world. From the minute he awoke until the time he finally went to bed, he was observing, learning, and growing. Anyone and everyone around him absorbed some of what he absorbed.

His life was his work, and by bringing that work home with him, his family became a part of that. Whether it was his fascination with anything on the airwaves, his business meetings or brainstorming sessions in the living room, or his rambling dictations often made sitting by the family pool (they had a pool next to their Manhattan penthouse) the man was alive and possessed by a creative energy that was both rare and seemingly without end. He believed that all of his new ideas would work. He also wanted to crowd as much living as possible into whatever time each day offered. Living to him meant making statements and waking people up to new things.

Unlike most children who never see their parents do anything that seems to change the world, Susan Weaver saw her father rewrite old ideas with new concepts every day. Here was a man who believed that anything was possible, and naturally passed that belief along to others. How could she help but feel that way, too?

Pat Weaver was also someone who never wanted to stagnate or be bored. Because of this his family benefited from new and exciting experiences. It might be a new type of food, tickets to a creatively off-the-wall play, or moving every four months. Whatever it was, life was never dull. And certainly, because of the money in the family, they were never short of the funds to do whatever they wanted to do.

Young Susan's life, and the wealth that had come with it, also kept her from seeing the real world where other children lived. She didn't know what it was like to want for a toy and not have it. She didn't feel the pressure of parents who wanted to give their children so much of the best but could never find a way to do it. She didn't play in parks or playgrounds or watch her mother wash and iron or her dad attempt to fix the family car on Sunday afternoons. In her own words, "I was a privileged, pampered, sheltered child." For her, every day had a happy ending and fairy tales did come true.

By not knowing the life of a normal child; by not ever hearing a parent shout exasperatedly, "I only wish I could do this or buy that"; by never seeing the negative world where "can'ts" are more a part of reality than "cans," Susan Weaver spent her early childhood years in a world usually seen only in movies. She was taught in private schools and given playmates who were living in the same kind of world to which she was accustomed. Happily isolated in this big bubble, reality rarely popped through and touched her.

But the days of Pat remaining a network god and public genius were numbered. His fall from grace began in 1954, when CBS was simply outdistancing NBC in the ratings. With each new ratings period the figures became worse. By 1956 the second network had only one show in the top ten. While it was true that *Today* and *Tonight* were doing well, by themselves they weren't going to be enough to save Pat's job. Prime time was simply not luring viewers or advertisers. Culture and ninety-minute spectaculars were not selling, and Pat Weaver did not want to give up on them. Ultimately, NBC bumped him up to chairman of the board and replaced him at programming with Robert Sarnoff.

As chairman of the board, Weaver did little except preside over meetings. He had no real imput into programming or the day-to-day operations of the network he had once run. He studied Indian religion and balanced on his bongo board to pass the time. Finally, after six months of boredom, he resigned in September of 1956.

NBC didn't fight his resignation. As a matter of fact, they gave a cash settlement of over $200,000 (a staggering sum at the time) just to help him out the door. He was a genius from the past, one they didn't need anymore. He had once been their savior; now he was simply a has-been.

The major news magazines covered his leaving with long stories filled with glowing tributes, almost as if he had died. But Pat Weaver was still very much alive and looking for new areas in which to contribute his insights. To him, leaving NBC was an escape to something better, not an end to his power.

Yet for a seven-year-old girl it meant that their world would be no more gold cards at Radio City, no more playing backstage, and no more fun evenings filled with people who would show up the next night on everybody's television. The circus had left town and the little girl must have mourned a little. Still, just as it was time for her dad to move on, it was time for Susan to grow up. And grow she would.

4

When Pat Weaver left NBC in late 1956, the family's standard of living did not change radically. NBC had paid dearly on the buyout of the former chief executive's contract, and the preceding generation's money had placed the family in a position of being very well-fixed. Still, it was the constant flow of exciting people and fresh ideas missed most keenly by the family. They no longer lived in the fairy-tale world of television royalty. They were back to being normal people with money.

Pat Weaver was still planning and dreaming big. He felt as though his ideas would and could work if only he had the exclusive power to do them the right way. In other words, he wanted to create television the Weaver way without interference from the old network guard. In order to do this, he spent a great deal of his time devising plans to put together a fourth network. Looking back at this time, Susan would remember that her father was working on ways to "transform" television. Unfortunately, neither the little girl nor the people who needed to be sold on Weaver's transformations could really understand him. While Pat Weaver still had great faith in what he was doing, too many others didn't. Times were far too conservative.

Meanwhile, Susan continued to grow in a world that mixed the wide-open ideas of her father with the conservative rich-girl schooling of a privileged young lady. She was obviously bright, very interested in learning, and way in front of the other children in educational maturity.

Rather than spending hours playing with dolls and toys, Susan read and dreamed dreams of being in wonderful places and accomplishing wonderful things. Even in grade school she didn't pause for hours entertained by *Nancy Drew;* she sunk herself into epics like *Moby Dick, Cinderella, The Nutcracker Suite,* and *Suddenly Last Summer.* And she just didn't read these books—she lived them.

One day she might be a rat, the next a mouse, the next a cannibal. Already, even before her teens, she was studying parts and becoming what she observed and read. She was an actress; reading, then acting out, was how she expressed herself. And like her father, she threw herself into her roles with all of her being. In any other family, a child who spent hours studying and then becoming a rat might spend a few sessions with a child psychologist. In the Weaver home, Susan was looked upon as being just one of the family.

Although the little girl still missed her trips to Radio City Music Hall and the other special places to which she had once been privy, she was growing and expanding much too quickly to pine for long. By the time she reached her teens, she was intelligent, cultured, and tall. The former two traits allowed her to stand out as a student in such prestigious schools as Manhattan's Brearley and Chapin. The latter forced her to stand out everywhere.

One of the things she really enjoyed doing

was taking her acting at home a step further. She excelled on the stage. It was her courage to do what ever it took, unlike that of many youngsters who allow their inhibitions to get in the way of acting, that allowed her to find some success as well as experience real fun. Her first role was that of Bottom in *A Midsummer Night's Dream.* That seventh-grade role led her to try out for others. She loved being someone else and experiencing whatever they were experiencing.

Acting was also a way to escape the emotionally painful realities of what her own body was doing to her. She had grown so quickly that by thirteen she was 5' 10", making her, quite justifiably, terribly awkward. She found herself the constant center of attention not only because she was a head taller than her friends but because she tended to be very clumsy, too. Because she was constantly being laughed at, and because she couldn't really help her own lack of coordination, she became a clown. Even she would later admit it was a defense mechanism. The key was that it worked, and she did make people laugh.

Yet the doors in New York simply weren't opening to Pat Weaver as they once had been.

Each year brought more rejection of his ideas on television programming. Rather than beat a dead horse (or perhaps running out of new apartments to lease) the Weavers looked west. They packed their bags and moved to San Francisco, California.

For Pat Weaver it was a trip back home. For his wife it was a chance to look at a new part of her adopted country. But for Susan, it was a shock.

For starters, she was shy. She had been raised in a protected cocoon and still did not truly know what it was like to mix with the real world. In New York society she had been socially and culturally protected; on the West Coast it was another story. Different elements of society mixed readily. Old money, status, previously established fame, and many other criteria that singled a person or a family out in New York meant nothing in California. You were judged simply by what you had done recently.

Susan was shocked by the girls she met. "I met girls who were twenty years older than I was who were my age," she has said when remembering that painful time. She was awkwardly out of step with the beach era and surfer girls. She didn't talk like they did, didn't listen to the same kind of music, have any interest in the games and clothes they wore; and with her height and curly, short brown hair didn't even look like she belonged. In her own words, she was an "ugly duckling."

Relating to members of the opposite sex was out of the question. She was too tall (far taller than most of them, anyway), too funny-looking, and too shy to get their attention. So, Susan lost herself in her beloved books, carrying on the roles of the characters who came to life as she read.

She didn't have to languish and suffer in the California sun for too long. Her parents decided to send her to the prestigious Ethel Walker prep school in Connecticut.

By wearing her school uniform, by once again mixing in with girls who came from equally rich and sheltered backgrounds, by escaping the real world, she found a place where she could stand out for the right reasons. She was a top student and an inquisitive yet well-mannered person. Both of those counted for a great deal at Ethel Walker.

Her days were filled with English literature, algebra, ancient history, and of course the traditional field hockey games that every New England boarding school seems to have.

Her nights were filled with studying and reading. It was a perfect world for Susan Weaver, except that she still stood a head taller than everyone else and was growing quite tired of being called "Susie." To her it seemed like such a little-girl's name, and one look could tell anyone that she was hardly a little girl anymore.

At the end of her freshman year, the upperclasswomen held a vote naming the still-awkward Susie as the "nerdiest girl in school." This hardly served as a boost for her confidence. Still, she was beginning to believe that there was something special about herself, and one evening, while reading F. Scott Fitzgerald's *The Great Gatsby*, she discovered the first step that would lead to her slowly changing from a caterpillar to a butterfly.

As the tormented Susie read a segment of the book, a passage about a party, she uncovered a character often overlooked and forgotten in Fitzgerald's most famous work. The character, an obscure aunt, is mentioned only once and never seen, but her name—Sigourney—mesmerized the young reader. The next day she informed the world that she was no longer Susan; from this day on her name would be Sigourney!

The kids at Ethel Walker slowly picked up on the "nerd's" new request. Her parents were a bit slower. They compromised by simply calling her "S."

By her sophomore year, Susan/Sigourney had graduated from her nerd status into the school's tallest "fairy queen." With her little gold tiara, she fluttered, as best a young girl of almost six feet in height could, around the campus waving a wand and throwing talcum powder on everyone during special occasions. It was a unique assignment, one which she took on with every ounce of her spirit and one which most of her friends would never have lowered themselves into doing. But then again, the Weaver kid was different.

By her junior year she was still flying, but this time as "Junior Birdman." This honorary title meant that she was the funniest girl in school. So the humor that had started as a way to play off her own height had finally given her a special kind of popularity. Now, on the special occasions where she had once fluttered around on her own, the other schoolgirls carried her on their shoulders and sang, "Up in the Air, Junior Birdman."

Unlike most class clowns, Sigourney was a serious student. But the scattered interests that so firmly marked her father had marked her, too. Other kids in her classes had special goals and plans. They wanted to act, teach, dance, or just get married. She wanted to do it all.

As a child Sigourney had spent many a day wrapping her arms around a literary character that had fascinated her the day before. In her teens she was still doing the same thing. She couldn't decide whether she wanted to be a doctor, a lawyer, or a marine biologist. She hovered, and somehow she hoped that she could find a way to do everything she wanted.

Meanwhile she would return home for the summers and do the usual things society girls did: go to parties, go to nice family gatherings by the ocean, and, of course, be a debutante. Sigourney was the tallest, and possibly the stiffest debutante at her coming-out party. All dressed in white, she hardly felt pretty or graceful, and yet those who witnessed the event swore that the strange little duck was beginning to look a bit more swanlike. But unlike the other roles that she so readily played, she really didn't care for that of *grande dame*. Every other girl's fantasy was not really hers. She preferred Junior Birdman.

One summer trip took the teenager and her family to Israel. Sigourney, the American WASP, loved the feeling of revolution and the special spirit that the relatively new country's citizens felt about this land they were building. She begged her parents to allow her to stay, to work with these people in reclaiming their wonderful history and carving out a new destiny. She even found a job working a potato-peeling machine on a kibbutz. On her first day she broke the machine, and was told that she wouldn't make a very good kibbutznik. So the WASP princess returned home, still wanting to help the "wonderful heroes" she had met.

It didn't take a Ph.D. to figure out that Pat Weaver's daughter was a romantic. She lived so much in that fantastical and idealistic world of her books that reality and what she was really going to do with her own life didn't seem to find much room or concern from her. She simply flew from role to role, from dream to dream, hovering for a moment, experiencing the sweetness of each new part and then flying on. She didn't seem to land anywhere for long.

gr1

school, at an age where a young lady was often expected to be grown up, could probably be traced back to how little of the real world Sigourney had actually experienced on a firsthand basis. It hadn't been a struggle for her, and except for her brief brush with the unique citizens of the world of California, her existence had been sheltered to the extent that she probably saw no reason to be too serious about herself and every reason to believe and be serious about idealistic causes. Unless you have seen firsthand ideals be ground down by reality, it is difficult to even stop to think that victory doesn't always belong to the good and that everyone has exactly what they've always wanted. Sigourney had no reason to believe otherwise; she had not been in contact with those who struggled for sheer survival. She had lived in an idealistic world where losing a job didn't mean losing all your money, your home, and your food. No matter what happened, no matter how soon she decided to get serious about her life, she was secure, with no real need to worry about the things that really mattered. Her close friends didn't either. And

She knew all the important current events, and she could see that her father was still wheeling and dealing and very much in the press and the public eye. The latter was probably far more interesting to her. With much hoopla, Pat Weaver had sold people on the idea that pay television would work. He was convinced that people would pay a nominal fee to have this television system cabled into their homes in order to view things like opera, plays, and sporting events. In 1965, the world didn't buy it in numbers to make it pay off. Pat had swung and missed again. Just as he'd tried to do at NBC a decade earlier, Pat had a great idea but not the best way to use it. He was still too much of a visionary. Ironically, a decade later his ideas were refined and packaged with less high-brow culture and the common man bought it. Cable television is now as commonplace as network television.

In their home in Santa Monica, the Weavers were tasting the bitter fruits of an idea man's ideas not being good enough. Pat Weaver was not the kind of person who could rest on his laurels on merely being considered a genius for creating *Today* and *Tonight*. He still wanted to be at the forefront of media creation. Still, the defeat of his fourth network while still on the drawing board, and then his pay TV concept failing within months of its conception didn't beat down his self-confidence. He continued to believe in what he was doing, and he was going to keep on doing it.

Meanwhile, Sigourney was less believing in what she was doing than believing she could do everything. Her focus was wide—too wide, thought many of her teachers. She wanted to be in every play and read every book. She also wanted to save the whales and teach poor children. Her teachers were unable to convince her to really commit to anything specific, though this is hardly unusual for a college-bound student, so they steered her into a concentrative study of English, hoping that she would use her unparalleled skills of "getting into a story" by becoming a teacher. To Sigourney, this sounded like it could be fun and, of course, fulfilling. (Every serious high school senior wants to be fulfilled and important.)

At this point in her life, all hell had broken lose in the nation. Race riots and civil causes had given way to war protests and draft-card burnings. The war in Vietnam was a reality soon to tear America to pieces, and young people—kids the same age as the idealist Sigourney—became increasingly involved in the effort to stop the killing in a conflict they didn't understand.

At Ethel Walker, reality was very much what it had been a generation before. Yet with college just months away, Sigourney Weaver would soon find herself in the real world, and when she arrived, many of her idealistic ways would give way to a new understanding of life and her place in it. Of course, nothing would change overnight.

5

The late sixties were turbulent times for America, and they were especially times of great social upheavals among the country's thousands of college students. It was an era of sit-ins, violent riots, the hippies, acid rock music, discovery drugs, and free love. It was not a time of real beauty as much as it was a time of painful discovery. A nation, and many individuals within that nation, was beginning to feel less than perfect. For the first time in generations, young people were asking questions that couldn't be answered with the same old answers.

Nowhere were these feelings voiced to any greater extent than in the city of San Francisco. A large segment of the peace movement, and of course the most famous of the era's flower children, hailed from the City by the Bay. It was here, within this framework, that Sigourney Weaver now lived. And so, the young woman, recently reborn out of the proper and perfectly orchestrated world of private shows and debutante balls, found herself in the spontaneous world of 1967.

She had chosen to go to school at Stanford University. For a top student like herself it was a logical choice. The university had long been known for its educational excellence, and many of the nation's top professors and students from across the country had made this school their academic home for years. And while it well may have been the academic stature of the university that had helped her make her final decision, there was one more thing involved, too.

"I was tired of the East Coast, and Stanford offered me a chance to get away from it all," she explained. It also offered her a chance to move away from the rules, regulations, and guidelines of prep school, and jump into a school known for its open thinking and freedom of expression.

As her teachers had wanted, and even as her parents had hoped, the five-foot-eleven-inch freshman decided upon English as her major. With her usual degree of dogged determination and solid work habits, she began to earn excellent marks and impress her teachers. And she also found an atmosphere offering her more than just studies and girlfriends.

Sigourney was no longer the tallest person in every class. With her short dark hair and large eyes, she also no longer was an ugly duckling either. Her mother had helped her begin to see her real beauty even before she moved on campus. She convinced her daughter that she was stately. So, filled with a new-found confidence, the young lady moved across campus with her own kind of elegant grace.

It didn't take long for her long legs and quick wit to impress people, especially men. Sigourney found herself dating, and she also found herself liking the idea of being considered a good-looking woman, not simply a tall clown. Her height, long a major problem, became a point of pride for the young woman. She still stood out, but it was more as a swan than as a sore thumb.

Simply because the real world had discovered the real beauty in Weaver, and because she was in the middle of campus demonstrations and social upheaval didn't mean that she immediately changed into a new person. She remained idealistic and a little naive. She was, after all, a rich girl in a place filled with not only top students, but a lot of other kids from moneyed backgrounds as well.

Within months she had decided to not only become an English major, but to continue her studies until she received her Ph.D. Then, she would take all of this learning and extol the beauty of Shakespeare and Browning in a manner that all students might find fascinating.

Who knows what might have happened if she had stayed locked into this kind of thinking and not branched out in her work in the theater. She might have become a tall, lanky, female version of the eccentric professor cliché, wearing horn-rimmed glasses, carrying stuffy old books filled with equally stuffy old poems under each arm, and living on rice cakes, wheat germ, and various varieties of rare English teas. But the lure of the stage was still in her blood, and she responded by joining a theater group and taking a few drama courses.

By 1968, Sigourney was a sophomore, and she had established herself as a bright student with a flaky kind of personality. She was not only someone who could be depended upon to always make an "A" and take great class notes, but she was also someone who was considered a bit out of step with the normal student body. Just as she'd done as a child, she was carrying her reading—and now her acting—over into her life. In other words, she was becoming the latest thing she had read or acted.

In the conservative world of college in the late 1980s this behavior would have labeled her as a complete loony, but twenty years ago it was far easier to blend in. It was almost difficult to be considered strange in the middle of a cultural revolution whose theme was "Do your own thing." Everywhere you looked, this coming-of-age bunch of baby boomers was pushing fashion, morals, and music to the limit. Free thinking had led to free love and an awareness that money was not the only reason to live. Here was a generation attempting to shock all of the previous generations in almost every facet of their lives. Hence, one tall girl's actions and way of living out her fantasies hardly seemed to cause as much as a small ripple when taken in the atmosphere of the era.

These cultural attitudes and the freedom they allowed gave Sigourney an escape from her rich-girl past. Money was no longer a hindrance when it came to being judged or being accepted. She was just one of the guys. At no other period in recent history could she have so easily left behind the aura of prep school and the social trappings of her monied upbringing. Twenty years later she would have been judged and placed within a certain predetermined status group due to her elevated background, but in the late sixties a person was judged by what he or she was at that exact moment in time. Any young person could remove his or her past as easily as changing a shirt. For the first time in her life, Sigourney was known as her own person, not Pat Weaver's daughter. And she quickly learned how to best express her new freedom—on the stage.

Sigourney joined a community acting group and performed in classic plays such as *The*

Tempest and *King Lear,* though the productions were hardly classics. If anything they were quite irreverent. She earned good marks as an actress in these productions, but she wanted to stretch into a world with even fewer rules and boundaries than anything based on the standard or the norm.

So, leaving the world of plain, old theatrical productions, she joined a group of young actors who toured the Bay Area in a covered wagon, performing comedy in the various places they would stop. Filled with spontaneity and encumbered by few rules, this was the kind of drama that really appealed to Sigourney. She was experiencing the excitement of creating in much the same manner as her father had discovered it first in radio and then in television. Enabled to create her own characters and interpret each of them in her own way, she loved the immediate reaction of the crowds as well as the knowledge that she had the fate of her character and therefore herself in her own hands.

At this point her parents began to notice that their daughter was interested in something more than becoming an English professor. Both veterans of the business, they attempted to offer her some solid advice.

"They didn't want me to go into it. They thought it was a tough business and they didn't think I was tough enough." But just as she had gotten her height from her father, she had also gotten his desire to create, to open new worlds and make her own rules as she had always watched him do. And just as she had received her delicate yet strong beauty from her mother, she had also received that woman's love of the stage and an audience. The beckoning call of show business was beginning to hook Miss Weaver for good.

Still, Sigourney's ultimate performance was yet to come. In 1969 she began acting with another group. They called themselves guerrilla performers and they used their acting to focus the audience onto topical problems. At the time, the gravest problem facing the country was Vietnam. So this small troop began to act out various antiwar messages on the stage. In their own way, they put together protest messages that they hoped would fire people into action.

Sigourney found the group fascinating. They were not only creating their own work, but what they were creating had a message. It was a message she bought, too. The war in Southeast Asia had to be stopped. Americans could no longer be killed for no practical purpose.

In May of 1969, Sigourney Weaver found the true power of the stage and performance. She also began to understand just how much an actor's portrayal in a part can influence an audience.

The guerrilla theater group was staging a play called *Alice in ROTCland* at the Stanford football stadium. It was part of a large anti-war protest, and thousands of students attended. At a key moment in the presentation, the lead—Sigourney—was supposed to stand up, produce a copy of Mao's *Little Red Book* of sayings, and signal the start of a demonstration against America's overt military attitude abroad. All went well until Sigourney attempted to find the book. Frantically she searched in her tote bag, but it wasn't there. After buying the book, studying what it had said, and helping to figure out just where and how it was to be used in the skit, she had forgotten to bring it with her. As all great actresses would have done in her situation, she improvised. Grabbing her New York address book, she waved it in the air, quoted enough sayings to move her audience into not just a simple protest—but one in which her patrons would storm out of the stadium and burn Stanford's ROTC building to the ground.

As the building, now a worthless pile of cinders and ashes, smoked, the actress wondered how long it would be before she was either arrested for instigating a riot or simply asked to leave school on one of any number of charges. For a while, she was afraid to answer the phone or the door, but nothing happened. The administration was not amused, but they didn't single out Pat Weaver's daughter as a scapegoat. Meanwhile, on campus she had become somewhat of a hero. For Sigourney, the attention her part had given her was both frightening and thrilling.

While her role in *Alice* had helped her see the power acting can provide and made her want to keep her free time focused on the theater, within a year she had tired of the political movement. After all, what could compare to getting an audience so worked up that they burned down a building? It was a hard act to follow, and she found the inspiration was not there anymore.

In a way she was following in the footsteps of her father. Jump into something with both feet, have a big success with it, and then move on. She was always looking for something new, something to push her to a new high or open a new world.

By 1971 she left her *Little Red Book* and protest days behind. In the process she left reality behind, too. Moving into a young man's treehouse—yes, a treehouse—she began to dress as an elf. They wore matching elf suits in a variety of colors. It was hard to miss either of them as they walked across campus, but with her height, Sigourney particularly stood out in her predominantly red and blue costume, complete with hat.

While other parents had to contend with a daughter living with someone (as opposed to marriage), the Weavers had to get used to the idea that their daughter, the world's tallest elf, lived at an address that only Tarzan or the Swiss Family Robinson would find normal. Not only that, but she ate vegetables that had been appropriated from the university's experimental gardens. And the man with whom she was sharing a treehouse was also an elf. Despite the fact that Sigourney's parents had really not wanted her to go into acting, they must have experienced some relief when she announced that she was going to apply to the Yale School of Drama.

Even while Sigourney was up in her tree,

she hadn't sluffed off in the classroom. Far
from it. Elf suit or not, she was not to be
laughed at as a student. For her entire four
years at Stanford she had taken her education seriously, even while she pursued her
range of unusual extracurricular activities. Yale
was impressed with her transcript and her
breeding. They wanted Sigourney and accepted her without question. Of course they
did overlook one small detail, and when the
future Stanford graduate received her con-
firmation of admittance to Yale she immediately noticed what that was.

Dear Mr. Sigourney Weaver:
We are happy . . .

In Yale's mind, Sigourney was a man. She
soon straightened them out on that point,
even though there would be a few other things
she would never be able to get them to understand about her. (Their loss, of course.)

As Sigourney's life in sunny California
wound down, and as the elf received her degree, she formed a theater troupe of her own
and hit the streets of Los Angeles. She named
her group "The Birds," and as is almost always the case with birds, the group spent
most of its time in parks. While the experi-

ence did get her out of her treehouse, and while it did, once again, give the actress/director/writer a chance to feel the freedom of wide-open performing, it did not really offer her anything more in the way of success than her other open-air productions. It was more of a case of marking time until the move back to the East Coast.

While Sigourney looked forward to challenging Yale's outstanding drama department, her parents, past teachers, and friends were all attempting to talk her out of going into the theater. Various people suggested everything from law to her original plans of earning a doctorate in English, but she didn't or wouldn't listen.

Stanford had opened up a new world to her. She had found the freedom to express herself; she had learned how to relate to some very normal people; she had acted and created in ways that she had only done privately as a child; and she had challenged a bit of the real world and won. Much as her father had discovered in his early life, she decided that there were no limits to what she could do. She had developed a need to explore all the different facets of life. Drama allowed her to be all things, to experience all things and to live in all times without being considered "out to lunch."

While she found freedom as an adult in the world of college, she had discovered real freedom in the world of acting. And the creative freedom of acting would fuel her soul.

6

"I thought I'd have the opportunity to play a variety of different roles at Yale, but my teachers never cast me as anything except little old ladies. I didn't get to do anything that I could normally be expected to play in the real world."

Yale was not the wonderful, exciting, learning, and growing experience for which Sigourney had hoped. Instead, it was a hard lesson in perseverance, rejection, and personal questioning. For the very first time in her life, Sigourney Weaver found herself in a situation where not only was life not fun at the present, but nothing enjoyable looked like it would be coming her way in the future either.

She didn't make a good first impression on the faculty, and often it is that first impression that counts for so much in acting. In retrospect, it probably would have been better for Sigourney if she had showed up in something other than the elf garb that had been her trademark at Stanford. The Ivy League wasn't quite ready for that, nor were there a large number of treehouses to rent at Yale.

Overnight she had gone from the liberal and expanding West Coast to the conservative and staid traditions of the East Coast. She had traded experimental attitudes for tradition and heritage. She had returned to familiar territory only to find herself completely lost.

Sigourney had been used to trying any and everything she had wanted. At Stanford, as well as in the other groups with whom she'd worked, there'd been no limits, and little that had ever been out of reach. Any play, no matter how complicated, could be attempted.

It was a way for actors to grow and stretch. At Yale it was much different.

The Yale School of Drama was run by Robert Brustein. No one had ever questioned his credentials for his position, nor should they, for his reputation spoke for itself. He was in charge of the school because he was the very best. But his rules were very different than those at less well-known programs.

True to its reputation as a school, the Yale drama department was first and foremost intellectual. There were reasons for doing things and there were reasons for the way things were done; spontaneity was not a necessary aspect of the classical theater.

Sigourney was much like the New York City playground basketball player who suddenly finds himself attempting to make Bobby Knight's disciplined Indiana basketball team. She was long on the type of experience the coach found worthless and short on the fundamentals the coach deemed necessary. In a way, she was like a wild animal that had been trapped, brought to the zoo, caged, and fed. She could look around and see opportunities, but she couldn't seem to escape and hunt for them properly.

Her classmates included Meryl Streep, who

seemed to land many of the roles Sigourney wanted, and a host of other young would-be actors who had already learned the fundamentals of the theater inside-out. They knew the classics, and rather than make fun of them as Sigourney had in many of her productions, they treated them reverentially, like fine china. Many of her classmates didn't as much want to change the theater and do new things as they wanted to maintain a standard of doing things the way they had been done for hundreds of years.

Sigourney had too much of her father in her to understand and fully appreciate people who resisted change and new ideas. As she settled into her constant study of old works and largely backstage or minor onstage roles in productions, her views on her craft began to change. Suddenly acting was no longer the great adventure, constantly challenging the mind and opening new horizons. It wasn't a way to become everything a person ever wanted to be, all things at the same time. Most of all, it wasn't as much a fantasy as it was hard work.

Pat Weaver had told his daughter time and time again that it was a tough business, a business filled with disappointment and hardship. He had also told her that the twenty thousand dollars he was investing in her acting classes would buy nothing, but a law degree from the same school would provide her with a career. Perhaps Pat Weaver, once an idealistic man who knew no limits, didn't want his daughter to run into the same locked doors he had found.

"Joyless!" That is the way she has remembered her actual schoolwork. For the first two years, each semester evaluation would find her teachers suggesting that she find another career. It was something she must have often considered.

There was more to her casting problems than an initial impression made by an elf suit and a lack of serious theater background. She had blossomed into a stunning young woman, quite a head-turner. Everywhere she went people noticed her first for her beauty—but at Yale such an attribute was not the sign of a serious actress. Anything resembling "glamour" cost you. Not only could you not trade in on a pretty face and good figure, but if you had either, it was better to disguise them. Men and women with "movie-star good-looks" were considered airheads.

The other contributing cause leading to

Sigourney being turned down for part after part was her height. The actors were often much shorter than she was. A tall woman simply couldn't play a part with a shorter man. It seemed to be a rule drawn up especially to keep Sigourney off the hardwood and far away from the spotlights.

By her third year she had all but given up on becoming an actor. Instead, she transferred to the playwriting department, mainly showing up in plays as prostitutes (it seemed they could be tall and beautiful). In some ways, the playwriting classes were limited, too, but only by the professors. In the confines of these classes Sigourney met some of the best and brightest people she had ever known, and unlike the more rigidly classical actors, these students wanted to expand, create new methods of expression, and were open to Sigourney and her wild ideas.

So, after years of hearing little more than rejection and discouraging reviews from fellow students and professors, she was suddenly receiving wonderful feedback from people who were dreaming of writing the material that, someday, she wanted to take to the stage. Just as she was about to exit from a theatrical career, she walked through one door and found a creative outlet. Like her father, she couldn't survive without that outlet.

The best of her new friends and comrades were Albert Innaurato, Wendy Wasserstein, and Christopher Durang. All three of them went on from Yale to immediately establish themselves as successful playwrights in New York theater. And Christopher Durang became not only a friend, but a mentor and collaborator on several plays. It was he who really began to help Sigourney believe in herself and her talents again.

Sigourney's playwright friends helped her rediscover a zest and a joy that the confines of Yale's curriculum had taken from her life. She now had someone to drink with, laugh with, and most importantly, people who loved spontaneity as much as she did. Many of her days in the classroom were still miserable times surrounded by people who saw and wanted the world to be run in black and white and with strictly followed rules, but at night she had new friends who wanted to see just how far they could stretch reality.

Durang loved the tall, crazy girl as only a director/writer could love her. He saw her potential and range; unlike most of the others at Yale who felt she should stick with her earlier decision to be an English teacher, he believed she could be a great stage actress. Of course at this time, Durang's brilliance was not as well received as that of some of the more conventional directors at the school of drama. He was as off the wall as the actress herself.

Durang began to write wildly imaginative plays, almost experimental in nature, and in these unique productions he nearly always created a part for Sigourney. In one of them he cast her as a schizophrenic who kept a hedgehog under her skirt. This play proved to be a bit too much for theatergoers, and very few people actually saw it. Still, Sigourney was playing a role that allowed her imagination to soar, and it was easier to accept a failed play if it provided satisfaction.

For Sigourney, it was Durang who turned Yale from a test of survival into a wonderful experience. "Chris was always very supportive to me, even when other people were saying I shouldn't go into the theater. He and a few other friends were very good to me." Without Chris, it is possible that she might never have reconsidered acting again, but through his friendship, her creative juices once again began to flow.

Together they began to write. A lot of the stuff was just fun stuff, lines they liked but didn't really think would set Broadway on its ear. But this burgeoning spirit seemed to turn Sigourney's attitude and direction around, and her last year at Yale began to be a time of real growth.

With Durang's encouragement, she began to throw herself into the theater much as she had with her childhood books and plays. She did it for the only good reason she knew: the sheer joy of it. It didn't hurt that she and Durang always seemed to be discovering something new they had in common, either.

"We were in a singing class together, and that's where our cabaret show [another joint project written and presented while at Yale] came from. We both liked the same odd songs or we liked hearing normal songs in an odd way—changing them just a little bit so that they were weird." The results of that initial work eventually turned into a Berthold Brecht parody entitled *Das Lusitania Songspiel*, finished and successfully presented some years later.

Thus, Sigourney and Durang attempted to make a staid and starched Yale audience laugh at not only what the two writer/performers had written, but at themselves, too. They were two very different people—a woman almost six feet and considered too tall to be a leading lady, and a man barely five feet six inches, considered too short to be a leading man— but together they seemed to fit. They fit so well that even some of the professors and coaches who had discounted Sigourney's talents were beginning to tell her that she had promise as an actress.

Sigourney's years at Yale were like a typically written play. In the first act the innocent but self-confident young girl, full of dreams and plans, arrives from far away only to be treated with disdain by those around her. She doesn't fit in, but she is allowed to stay, although she is discouraged at every turn and often considers giving up.

In the second act, she is pushed even further down. Her misery now shows on her face, and her once creative mind has been affected. She is no longer engaged as much in an attempt to be loved and discovered as she is in a struggle to survive. The innocence is gone, and she has become an underdog in the true sense of the word. Even her belief in herself is slipping.

Finally, in act three, she meets someone who sees that sparkle, that zest for life that she had all but forgotten she once had. With his help she rediscovers herself and her happiness, forgets and overcomes the handicaps that others had imagined, stars in a few productions, shows those who had once put her down that she really does have star potential, and exits at the top of her world, beliefs intact and herself redeemed!

Actually, Sigourney didn't exit as "the" star. But she did finish with a great amount of respect from a number of those who had once thought her a round peg in the rather square world of Yale.

During the very proper graduation ceremony marking the end of her career at the Ivy League school, Sigourney proved to the world that she was leaving as she had come—with a flair. Dressed in a blue blazer and very conservative skirt, she unbuttoned the blazer at the end of the ceremony to reveal a large target placed over her heart. She drew a round of laughs.

Still, that stunt symbolically represented exactly what she must have felt during most of her days at Yale. She had been a target for ridicule and putdowns. She had been constantly told that she couldn't make it and should give up and go home. And through the entire three years, she had taken all the shots, and her spirit had not been broken. She left believing in herself and her creative abilities.

Still, Yale had accomplished one thing. Despite the success she had achieved with Durang and her belatedly appreciative reviews, Sigourney decided to give up acting as a career. The real joy of the craft had been taken from her by the rules and fundamentals required by serious acting. For Sigourney Weaver, freedom was important, and she saw very little future for herself in the theatrical arts.

A special last laugh . . .

Some years after Sigourney left the Yale School of Drama, she was asked to return to star in one of the school's productions. She was too busy working at her craft to honor the request. Yale now wanted Sigourney Weaver's name on the top of the bill, but it was a few years too late.

7

"When I left Yale it was my intention never to be a part of show business. I wanted a nice ordinary job."

Imagining Sigourney Weaver as a school-teacher or a bank teller tends to boggle the mind. The tall, bewitching beauty is not the person you would expect to see sending report cards home with a high school freshman. Still, the grind, competition, and general lack of success she had experienced at the Yale School of Drama had positioned her in a posture of a disillusioned twenty-five-year-old woman. The last thing on her mind was attempting to move on to the New York stage scene. She'd already endured enough rejection for one lifetime.

The one saving grace of Yale had been the special friends she had made in her playwriting class. Unlike her, they hadn't let the school's constant criticism stop them from moving on and seeking their dreams. It is possible that without the positive feedback and encouragement of these friends, Sigourney might never have finished school. There is no doubt that without them she would not have continued her acting career after graduation.

In 1975, Sigourney regarded acting and show business much as her father did—he referred to it as "the racket." And after she completed drama school he once again voiced this strong opinion, "If you had spent three years at Yale Law School instead of Yale Drama School, you could be starting at twenty thousand dollars a year."

Obviously, the elder Weaver's point was not really about money; after all, that had never been a family problem. The point centered upon wasting time, which was certainly something he didn't believe in. He was a mover and a shaker, and having a daughter who was wondering and wandering must have been a trial for his patience.

Even ten years after their daughter had rechristened herself with an outlandish name, her parents had problems with it; they still often called her simply "S." Perhaps she was too shy and too fragile for the industry that had been their lives. Both Weavers knew first-hand what it was like to be berated; to be constantly rejected; to be told that either you, your ideas, or your work were not good enough and never would be. They knew that even people with very thick skins had trouble deal-ing with this kind of treatment, and often they cracked under the pressure. Loving parents don't want to see their offspring immerse themselves in such a world, and certainly the Weavers didn't. Their son had become a salesman, and they hoped their daughter would use her considerable talents in an equally normal field.

As she packed her bags to leave Yale, Sig-ourney may have agreed with them. Her graduate studies had not been a waste, but they had also not been a joy. The years of elf garb and student demonstrations, of idealism and romance, probably seemed a million years behind her, and the future was a question mark.

But her friends had not forgotten about the girl thought by the Yalies to be too tall and too beautiful. Her unique abilities jumped into mind as Christopher Durang put together his latest play, this one scheduled for off-Broadway. He called Sigourney and offered her a part. *The Nature and Purpose of the Universe* was not to be a play that would rank with *Romeo and Juliet* but it was what kept Sigourney Weaver from quitting her chosen profession. In a way, this play is historically quite important in the life of an actress and the lore of Hollywood.

Certainly when Durang called, Sigourney's heart must have jumped a little. After all, he had been a large part of what had been good about Yale. But in the back of her mind there had to be the notion that acting in his play was merely a way to kill a few more months, and all that would come out of it would be more disappointment and wasted time. Maybe it was time for her to get on with her life in the real world.

Durang convinced her it wasn't. He didn't want her simply because he was her friend;

he had no shortage of old friends who needed acting roles. He wanted her because he saw her potential.

Soon, the young actress's doubts about her craft were to disappear, and she began to rediscover her own love of being onstage. The joys and the thrills were back with the rush of excitement of a real, live opening night.

"I realized that I could either have a terrible time opening night, or a good time. In a sense it was such a celebration at the show. 'Out of the gate,' that I was just gonna have a wonderful time."

The next three years were spent constantly auditioning. The rejection Sigourney had experienced at Yale would serve her well, for she was most often turned down. Many of the reasons were the same she'd heard before. She was too tall and too beautiful. Still, she believed enough in what she was doing to enjoy the moments when the auditions didn't go well. It was scary, constantly entering new theaters and meeting new directors, but it was a challenge, too.

"I don't think you can be fearless, but you have to use the fear as a kind of energy. It's like stage fright; I had a teacher who said, 'If

you're not nervous before a show, worry!'
That's adrenaline. I sometimes miss those
days where I could walk in off the street and
audition for something, and no one knew who
I was. I could just take over the role for five
minutes and do whatever I wanted and it was
all so honest."

This honesty, something that she had not
experienced in some time, must have appealed to her greatly. She had found a place
where she could be herself, and not have to
worry about what people thought of her. She
wasn't starving like other struggling artists—
and her background gave her a certain security that girls just arriving from the farm
in Kansas didn't possess—but she was experiencing what it was like to do it all on her
own.

Once she had tried to use the family name
to get a door opened, but the man she called
(a friend of her father's) suggested instead
that she seek employment at a department
store. In other words, the Weaver name was
not going to get her anywhere. Only her talent and ambition would determine if she flew
or fell as an actor.

With an energy her father had once em-
ployed while building a network, Sigourney

continued to make the rounds, looking for work. She had discovered that she was only happy when plying her trade, so her search for parts took her from theater to theater, off-Broadway, way-off Broadway, and even to regional playhouses. Sigourney wanted to prove herself. She read every posted bulletin, every casting call, and digested every ad in every paper. There were plenty of roles, but only a few people who earned them actually got them. It was a feeling that has stayed with her.

"It seemed for three years I was just sort of doing showcases in New York. I was lucky to get the showcases. I remember very vividly what all that uncertainty was like and every time I go to the public theater and they say, 'General auditions, upstairs,' I still feel a knot in my stomach because I remember how hard it was to get one, how much I went into it, and how always anticlimactic it felt after months of waiting and working."

The feeling of being rejected is something most actors never lose, and in New York those experiences unfortunately happen on an extremely regular basis. Still, what Sigourney had learned at Yale about sticking with what she believed in was beginning to become very important. In a way, life in the real world combined the harshness of her drama school experience with the freshness of the lack of limits of Stanford.

"At drama school they told me not to even pursue a career, so I had been so fundamentally rejected before I got to the city that I found the city a playground of opportunities. I could read in the paper about things, and go and audition for them. To me New York was the Promised Land. No one could say, 'No, you can't audition for that, you're going to play an old woman this time.' There was no dictator suddenly; and I found that very exciting. I had nothing to lose. I had already been told the worst. So, I think in an awful way, that was a great asset. I have other friends who were made much of at Yale, who had a much harder time adjusting, because people didn't stand up and say, 'Wow, you're the next so-and-so.' It took them longer, and I think one of the reasons is that I had no expectations. I got discouraged, but I didn't give up. I'd been given up on two years before that, so I really stayed in the business out of spite for awhile."

For every month Sigourney stuck it out, working in a hit-or-miss fashion, another group of promising actors with whom she'd gone to school gave up. They packed their bags and went on to another profession or to teach drama in high schools. The rejection they had rarely experienced in school proved to be too tough for them.

And for Sigourney the parts began to come more often, and with each new role she began to work with better and better professionals. The key was she didn't limit herself to a certain kind of role or production. She tried anything, and was scared of nothing.

After her initial appearance in Durang's *The Nature and Purpose of the Universe*, she worked in his double-bill, *Titanic* and *Das Lusitania Songspiel*. In *Titanic* she played a woman with multiple personalities. The part was difficult, and let her display her wide range of talent. Critics began to take notice, and good reviews led to more work.

She spent time on the stage of Joseph Papp's theater, and then appeared off-Broadway in plays such as *Gemini*, *Marco Polo Sings a Solo*, and *New Jerusalem*. In *Marco Polo*, she gained a great deal of recognition due to her costars—Joel Grey, Madeline Kahn, and Anne Jackson. To get an idea of how bizarre this play was, realize that Sigourney played a maid who cleans the glacier serving as the focal point of the drama's action. Later in the play, when she is artificially impregnated by an astronaut, her tummy lights up. It was hard for theatergoers to forget a role like that or the actress who brought it so masterfully to life.

After this she moved on to television, landing a part on *The Best of Families*, and then a recurring role on the soap opera *Somerset*. In the latter she played a polished young woman who had ambitions of becoming the nation's first female president. She also had a major part in John Cheever's PBS drama, *The Sorrow of Gin*, then landed a walk-on part in Woody Allen's *Annie Hall* (you see her outside a movie theater with Woody Allen, at the end).

Perhaps Sigourney's best chance to view a star who had already suffered many of the same "handicaps" that seemed to plague her career arrived when she served as understudy in *The Constant Wife*. Here was a production that toured the country and then landed on Broadway. It was directed by Sir John Gielgud, and the star was the tall and beautiful Ingrid Bergman. Ms. Bergman was not only an actress who could teach a young understudy a great deal, but she was a woman of independent nature and above-average stature who had beaten the odds to become a star of the highest magnitude. Certainly, here was a woman, a role model made to order for Sigourney.

Although she was gaining valuable experience and beginning to make her mark, the Yale School of Drama graduate and survivor had not yet hit that point where she could rest assured that earning a living as an actor was possible. Far from it. Despite her many roles in so many different arenas of the theater and television, she was really still an alien to those who knew the New York drama scene. All that was about to change.

8

By this time, Sigourney's intense desire was to move on to roles that would both expand her as an actress and propel her into a status of being more than just another woman in another role. She wanted an identity.

Obviously, with her height as well as with the mere nature of a business where few people ever make their mark, the odds were against her. Still, used to the rejection, she trudged on to audition after audition, and sent her bio and portfolio to every casting agent she could find. Time passed and little really came of her inquiries.

As 1977 moved into 1978, the actress, now approaching the age of thirty, was fully aware of a combination of events happening in the world of cinema. A large number of older actresses, such as Jane Fonda, were landing parts they once would have been considered too old to play; and actresses barely in their twenties were getting shots in the unknown roles. There was a huge gap—made up of unknowns all around thirty years of age—between those two groups and few were considering them for prime roles.

The painful reality of Sigourney's situation was that she might never be given a chance to act in a meaty role in New York or Hollywood. Television soap operas and off-Broadway plays might be as high as she could go. For someone who had been so well-educated, even if she hadn't particularly enjoyed the experience, this had to be a cold slap in the face. Her critics and teachers at Yale were seemingly being proven right.

Meanwhile, unbeknownst to Sigourney, Walter Hill, David Giler, and Gordon Carroll had written and were producing a movie that would take *Star Wars* into an area of unexplored space. Harkening back to movie concepts of the 1950s, these three men had come up with a haunted house story set on a spaceship. They had been making plans for their ultimate "boo" flick.

They needed to cast someone as a survivor of the mission, someone who could be a kind of blue-collar, gritty hero. This was not going to be a John Wayne or Gary Cooper type of rescuer, but rather a working stiff who rises to the occasion in spite of himself. After looking at and considering actors throughout Tinseltown, they thought they had found their perfect Officer Ripley in Paul Newman. But Newman evidently didn't think so.

So the trio continued to search for actors to portray the lead as well as the six other crew members of the ship *Nostromo*. After a while they began to consider that in the faraway future women might have reached a status of equality that would make an all-male crew seem a bit unusual. So they sat down and rewrote two of the parts for women, and their casting search began all over again.

Sigourney, not working very steadily anywhere, had moved to a basement apartment near the Hudson River on Manhattan's West Side. This was a place right out of an old

black-and-white television detective show
script. Not only did she have to contend with
the noise of the traffic and constant moans
of typical city life, but her apartment was
located directly across from the subway rail-
yards. Day and night, the cars would couple
and uncouple, screeching to a halt and rat-
tling the building. Needless to say, the rent
was not high. Nor was the length of stay of
most renters. The noise, ever constant and
not the least bit rhythmic, would drive people
crazy within weeks.

Sigourney described the place to her friends
as hell, and she was probably wondering if
her life was just about the same. Dreams of
big parts had now become hopes for *any* parts,
and the promise of a future filled with starring roles seemed even further out of reach.

One day, however, Sigourney returned
home to find a message asking her to call
Mary Goldberg. Goldberg was an independent casting agent, and she had become familiar with Sigourney's work. She told the
young actress she thought that she might
have something for her, and she arranged a
meeting with producers Hill, Giler, and Carroll.

The meeting with the men went well. They

were impressed with Sigourney's looks, her voice, and the way she carried herself. She was strong. For the role of Ripley they needed someone who was not a frail and fainthearted actress. This was not a glamorous role, and there would be no romance within the framework of the movie. Beauty wasn't important, but toughness was. After all, the actress who played the part would have to replace a Paul Newman type. It would also be easier for those viewing the film to believe in a woman they'd never seen before rather than an actress who had already created an image through her work. Sigourney, completely unknown to movie fans, seemed to possess all of the qualities to make audiences believe that she could be a survivor and a hero. At the end of the interview, the producers gave her a script and asked her to read it overnight. They wanted to see her again the next day.

In this meeting a fourth man, director Ridley Scott, joined the producers. They spent the next several hours discussing Sigourney's view of the part, looking at drawings of the sets, and discussing how each person believed the movie would work. When the meeting adjourned, they thanked the actress for coming, and offered her no real encouragement on the outcome of who was going to get the part. The producers and director went back to the West Coast, and Sigourney headed back to her depressing apartment and another round of general auditions for stage plays.

Weeks after she had first spoken with the film's director and producers, she once again heard from Walter Hill. He was back in New York and wanted to see her. In their meeting he informed her that everyone who had met her thought she was perfect for the film's central character, but she had to cross another hurdle before she could even test for the role. It seemed that Alan Ladd Jr., head of 20th Century Fox, had never heard of Weaver. He personally wanted to see her before spending the time and the money on a screen test.

The next day Sigourney was on her way to Los Angeles to meet with Ladd and the other executives at Fox. The coast-to-coast flight allowed her plenty of time to think about just how important this meeting would be for her future. If she impressed these people, she would land the starring role in a major studio's movie. If she blew it, she would be listening to the subway cars couple and uncouple and wondering if law or teaching wouldn't have been better suited for her after all these years.

As luck would have it, the airline lost her luggage. Her schedule was too tight to allow her the time to buy anything to wear, and she was forced to impress Ladd and the other executives in a simple tee shirt and a faded pair of jeans. Her attire seemed to matter little, and for the unglamorous part they were financing, it might even have helped. Ladd decided he wanted her in London in two days to test for the role.

Forty-eight hours later she was in England, preparing for a grueling day of testing. Jet lag or not, exhausted and hungry or not, she was given her directions, her lines, and a general introduction of what they wanted her to do, and then she was told to do it. With cameras rolling, she went to work in London's fabled Shepperton Studios. Beginning in early afternoon and not even stopping for tea, the British crew worked her until almost two the next morning. Then, they simply took her back to a hotel room and told her to get some sleep.

After all the hard work, sleep came easily.

As Sigourney prepared to head back to the States the next day, she also mentally prepared herself for the weeks or months of waiting that would be involved before she found out if she got the role. Needless to say, she was shocked when she received a call from the producers congratulating her before she even had time to check her flight schedule.

Within a month, she would have to be back in England filming *Alien*, a role that, only a few months before, had been marked for a male superstar. As is often the case in the crazy business of entertainment, just when all doors seemed closed, others appear wide open. But as is also the case with the business, just when doors often appear wide open, someone closes them.

Within days of announcing that the unknown Sigourney Weaver had the lead role in *Alien*, the studio found itself under fire in England. The members of the actors' union were demanding that Fox change the casting of the part of Ripley. They wanted a British actress in the role. An unknown actress could just as easily have been found in the country where the film was being made.

Since none of the starring roles had gone

back to locals, the producers could certainly understand the union's outcry. It did seem as though this trans-Atlantic film smacked of colonial prejudice in the casting department. Conciliatory meetings began, and Hill, Giler, and Carroll began to explain why they had to have Ms. Weaver as the star. Like a fight for a boxing title, each round brought a new charge and a counterattack. Finally, with the schedule to begin shooting just days away, the deadlock was broken.

Winning the lead in a movie called *Alien* must have seemed a bit ironic for Sigourney. An alien is just what she had seemed to be for most of her life. She had been born privileged, which had set her apart from the general public. In California she had been a prep school easterner in a beach-boy world. In college she had marched to a beat that was strange even in the anything-goes world of the late sixties and early seventies. In Yale, her height, her desire for expression, and her Stanford education had placed her in a position of being difficult to cast and often considered hopeless. On the stage she had almost always been too tall or too stunning. And most of all, she had always been too bright. For Sigourney, with the British up in arms because she wasn't from their country, she would once again be an outsider.

Despite all of this, when she left her apartment-on-the-Hudson for London on the last Saturday in June, she didn't seem the least bit nervous or worried about the reception she would face. She had already been hit with too much rejection to allow anything anyone else said or did bother her now. She had taken on the aura of her role as Ripley. She was already thick-skinned, tough, and ready for action. And, like Ripley, she didn't really know where an attack was going to come from next. When she arrived, however, the casting problems had been forgotten and no harsh words came at all.

The next several months of her life were spent in the suburbs of London. She was working, often twelve and more hours a day, in the land where her mother had acted. But while her mother had most often appeared in the theater, Sigourney was involved in a new-wave horror film of the highest magnitude. This film wasn't meant to make the audience cry or fall in love—it was meant to scare them to death. To that end, the largest and perhaps weirdest soundstage of all time had been constructed to resemble an eerie, dark spaceship and a strange, frightening world. Every set seemed to have been built so that there was always something lurking just out of view in the darkness.

It seemed as though every broken and used piece of machinery in London had been dumped in Shepperton Studios. Tunnels were constructed out of old plastic pallets, and mirrors helped make those tunnels seem endless. The spaceship had become exactly what the writers had intended—the world's largest haunted house—and the planet outside that ship had become the perfect stormy night. Besides the setting, the only difference between *Alien* and the Universal Studios horror epics of the forties and fifties was that what was hiding beyond the door wasn't a ghost or a monster—it was a creature from outer space.

The change of setting and the sophisticated technology utilized by director Scott took this B-movie plot and idea and transformed it into a masterful piece of film work. Far more than a "boo" movie, *Alien* was rather like one of Hitchcock's films, containing nail-biting suspense and believable characterizations.

For starters, the crew was not all-American

and good-looking. The ship they lived on looked like a huge garbage tug. And from the very beginning, nothing got in the way—not romance, fun and games, or cheap laughs—of letting anyone in the darkness of a movie theater relax for a single second. There was always something ready to jump out at you, hidden off-screen and just out of view.

Tom Skerritt, Veronica Cartwright, Harry Dean Stanton, John Hurt, Ian Holm, and Yaphet Kotto made up the motley crew, a bunch of second-rate losers. This wasn't a stellar team sent out to explore the exciting reaches of the universe, but rather a group of people who'd never really cut high enough marks to make the big time. There they were, stuck doing something most people would never want to do. They got dirty and greasy to make a buck, and Sigourney was one of them. Her character was no better, no more idealistic and goal-oriented. To all of these people, life wasn't as much a dream as it was a pain.

Perhaps because they were not hero-type material, we found ourselves at first not caring much about them. So what if a monster popped up and killed a few of these guys? They were headed nowhere. But because they were human beings, and despite the fact that they were not the kind we would want to have crashing in our guestroom, we slowly began to care about them. And when the creature exploded out of John Hurt's gut, we suddenly cared a great deal. The movie quickly took on an Us *vs.* Them mentality.

As the plot progressed, Sigourney's character developed into a person with a high degree of intelligence and class. She was someone who suddenly felt something for her crew members, and even the ship's cat. Maybe, the audience began to feel, there was more of a reason for us to root for her beyond the fact that she was someone like any one of us. We projected ourselves on to her character, and her portrayal was called strong and solid even by the critics who would pan the film. But as a whole, the reviews were fairly good.

David Denby in *New York* magazine wrote: "*Alien* is terrifying but not enjoyable. It works on your nerves and emotions like a torturer extracting a confession." In *The New York Times* Vincent Canby would say, "It is an old-fashioned scare movie about something that is not only implacably evil, but prone to jumping out at you when you least expect it."

"*Alien* is an old-fashioned scary movie set

in a highly realistic sci-fi future, made all the more believable by the expert technical craftsmanship that the industry just gets better and better at," were the words of *Variety*. On the other hand, Stanley Kauffman in *The New Republic* was a little disappointed. He stated, "It's a smash hit, but it might have been even smashier." Still, overall, the critics at least thought it better than the current crop of slasher movies.

For Sigourney the film became something far more important than a $35,000 paycheck and a ticket out of oblivion. For her *Alien* was the way to show her determination to command notice as a real actress, someone who could bring something to any and every role she played. She knew that as Ripley she would either live or die as an actress, so every bit of her substance went into the role.

London was a beautiful city, and summer festivals and long dusky twilights beckoned, but most of Sigourney's off-hours were spent studying and restudying her script. She wanted to know why her character did everything she did. She wanted to *become* Ripley, and in a way she did. As had her dreams as a child, this role began to consume her life. She was fighting an alien, she was an officer on a ship hauling ore across the universe, and she did care if she survived. If Ripley died, Sigourney knew that a part of her would die, too, and with every passing day she spent working with her character, the more she wanted Ripley to embrace the special qualities about which Sigourney herself cared most.

This unique approach to her work may have been caused by Sigourney's tendency to fantasize, consumed by those teenage dreams of being everything and doing everything; or perhaps by the discipline learned by a stage actress living a role every day for months and months. But its origin was not important as long as it got to us. Sigourney was Ripley and Ripley was Sigourney.

When the day came for her to film the climactic scene of the film—the part where she thinks she's won and exhaustedly prepares to board a shuttlecraft, take a shower, and head home—the writers and producers changed the script on her. No longer would she be nude when she fought the monster; she would be clothed in male-type underwear.

Sigourney was surprised. She felt her creature needed to be nude, to contrast the pink, fragile form of her own body against the monster's slimy exterior. She felt that it would be a shock for the creature to see her that way, and that shock would give her the time to blow it away.

Yet the fear of losing many members of the audience with a nude scene made the producers back off. (And judging by the mail Sigourney later received for appearing in a nearly nude state, perhaps America wasn't ready to view her in the all-together after all.) Still, her battle to keep what she believed to be right in the script certainly showed the cast and crew that this was not a typical Hollywood actress who read her lines and then forgot about them.

As the filming ended and the set was being torn down, the actors and crew said their goodbyes and packed their bags for home. The wrap of a motion picture is usually a time of relief as well as grief. Relief because the long hours are over and the hard work is a part of the past. Grief from knowing that when you leave the set for the last time, people you've met and come to know as friends will move on to other jobs and walk out of your life. And something even larger disappears with the last day—the character you portrayed. Most actors learn to accept that as fact, but Sigourney mourned that loss as much as she mourned losing her new friends.

Her first important role, Ripley, was gone. As Sigourney left England for her tiny New York apartment, she must have felt as though a friend had died. Little could she have realized what that "friend" would do for her career, or how Ripley would come back to life in the future. For now, Sigourney returned to the real world of Manhattan and the knowledge that for the next few months she wouldn't have to hunt for work. For the first time since Stanford, she could relax and enjoy life. She was looking forward to it.

9

After returning from England, Sigourney tried to go back to her usual routine, but she realized something quite unsettling was beginning to happen to her. With a starring movie role behind her, her friends were looking at her differently. The comfortable feeling that had once been there was gone. Success had given these friends a different perception of her.

She had seen countless colleagues from the theater who had gotten close to making a major film or doing a Broadway play, only to have their big break fall through at the last minute. Even her part in *Alien* had come close to ending before it began. She certainly knew about the fine line between success and failure. But the few who had made it hadn't returned to their old haunts—they had either packed their bags and moved to the West Coast, or they had taken out digs in a better part of town, leaving the past behind them.

Now, with a possible success under her belt, and a $35,000 paycheck in the bank, Sigourney wasn't considered one of the struggling actors anymore. She was no longer a true member of the fraternity that had once held her so dear.

She didn't like that, so instead of moving to a more amenable place she stayed in her apartment by the river. Instead of making the scene at the New York society parties, she continued to hit the local and more intimate parties of the people she had always known. And, most importantly, instead of kicking back her heels and resting, she went back to work in the same kind of parts and on the same kind of stages as she'd done since leaving Yale.

Sigourney wanted to improve, and improvement was gained through studying with acting coaches like Gene Lasko, Nikos Psacharopoulos, and Robert Lewis. She took dance from Carmen de Lavallade, and she and friend Christopher Durang began to write together again. She was growing, unlike many who simply believed that once you began to make a little money and have a little success, you could bank on what you'd done already.

Soon she and Durang were jamming again. They knew each others' rhythm so well that they could sense the timing it took to make a play work. Together they had won a Drama Desk award for *Das Lusitania Songspiel* for writing, as well as rave reviews for both of them as writers and actors in the production of that play at the Chelsea Theater. Sigourney's parody of Marylin Monroe brought the house down almost every night during the show's run. Now, in late 1980, they were working together on *Beyond Therapy*. The first play had been a critical success, and in the off-Broadway circles, *Beyond Therapy* would be a huge success, too.

Yet before Sigourney had become involved in the project, a great number of things had happened to place her in the New York spotlight, a spotlight she didn't like and almost always avoided. Even in interviews, she kept the public and private parts of life separated.

She had been very impressed in late 1979 with a play entitled *Lone Star*. Its young writer, James McLure, impressed her even more than the play had. He was good-looking, very bright, and talented. He challenged Sigourney's wit and mind, and they had immediately developed a passion for each other.

In the past her romantic interludes had gone largely unnoticed. Then, in mid-1979 when *Alien* had become the season's big hit, the newspapers were after everything they could find out about her. She had managed to keep them in the dark until she and McLure began seeing each other.

The critics had adored both of his Broadway plays. While not a huge box office hit, *Pvt. Wars* had marked him as a man to watch in the theater world. The mere fact that he was not attached also made him someone to watch on the streets. So within months of beginning to date, Sigourney and McLure had gone from being left alone in privacy to being sought. The public's fascination with her was based on a single movie, and with him it was based on two of his plays.

It was hardly surprising that they had fallen

At the 55th annual
Academy Awards
presentation, *left*,
held at the Dorothy
Chandler Pavilion in
Los Angeles. 1983.

© Star File

Sigourney, *below*, at
the screening of her
latest film "The
Year of Living
Dangerously." 1983.

© Ron Galella

*L*ooking as elegant as ever, *above*, with her parents, Elizabeth Inglis and Pat Weaver.

*C*igar smoking, *right*, with Mel Gibson at the party to celebrate "The Year of Living Dangerously". 1983.

*P*osing with MGM/UA Motion Picture President, Freddie Fields and co-star Mel Gibson at the screening of "The Year of Living Dangerously". 1983.

© Ron Galella

*I*n a scene from the Peter Yates movie, "Eyewitness" co-starring William Hurt.

© *Phototeque*

A scene from "The Year of Living Dangerously", *below*, the romantic adventure movie co-starring Mel Gibson, set against the background of the 1965 Indonesian civil war.

© Phototeque

*A*t the opening party of "Hurly Burly", *left*, in New York. 1984.

© Geoffrey Croft/Retna

*S*igourney with husband-to-be Jim Simpson, *left*, after the first preview performance of "Hurly Burly". 1984.

© Ron Galella

© Phototeque

$\int$igourney as Ripley, *above*, the starship's warrant officer, with Jones the cat in a scene from "Alien".

$\int$igourney as Ripley, *right*, in the wildly successful sequel, "Aliens" protecting Newt played by Carrie Henn against an army of deadly extraterrestrials. For her role in this movie, Sigourney was nominated for an Academy Award.

*O*ffstage or on, she's strong, competent, and self-assured. First and foremost, Sigourney is a one-of-a-kind, straightforward woman.

© Phototeque

*P*laying her famous siren role in a scene from "Ghostbusters" with Rick Moranis.

© Globe Photos

*P*osing for
photographers at
a meeting of the
Hollywood Foreign
Press Association.
1986.

*A*ttending the industry
screening of
"Aliens" with her
father, Pat Weaver.
With such a
beautiful, talented
daughter, no wonder
father looks so
proud. 1986.

for each other. He was fascinated by an actress who could not only act, but think. The fact that she was also a free spirit who was unimpressed with position while enjoying the company of people who believed they could touch rainbows and catch stars also must have turned his head. To say nothing of her beauty.

Meanwhile, Sigourney had always been drawn to people who were unafraid to express themselves honestly, and take their fate in their own hands, building their futures by bucking the odds. McLure had done that.

Their mutual love of the theater gave them hours of enjoyment. The time they spent together may have cemented the fact of just how much they not only had in common, but to how great an extent they were going to grow in the same direction.

Suzy, a gossip columnist for the New York *Daily News*, got wind of their affair and delivered the word in the late summer that the two lovebirds were sharing a roost together. It took passion rather than success to pull Sigourney out of her basement apartment.

Unfortunately, the romance was doomed from the beginning. Both Sigourney and McLure wanted to keep every private detail of their lives secret, but because both of them were successful they couldn't go anywhere without being noticed. It was reported in the press when they took an apartment on Riverside Drive; it was also reported that the apartment was so infested with fleas that they were forced to move out on the first day. After sending for an exterminator, it was reported that they moved temporarily to the Algonquin Hotel. Eventually, when their place was debugged, it was reported that they returned home.

Meanwhile the two of them were heading in different career directions. While being heralded as a great actress who would take Hollywood by storm, Sigourney was being offered parts calling for her to do little more than accompany a man or hang on his arm. She was being offered no starring role, nothing with any meat.

"Most of the roles I was offered after *Alien* were cute, sassy little satellites to the leading male character. They twinkle briefly and then fade away. The general thinking seemed to be that I was a big enough name to team with a major male star in a kind of combo situation. But invariably the story centered on the man, not the woman."

At the same time, McLure was trying to

not only write the followups to his critically acclaimed first works, but to keep those works alive. The reviewers loved them, but they were not drawing the crowds to the theater. The savior of both of their lives appeared to be film director Robert Altman.

Altman had loved McLure's *Lone Star*, and had gone so far as to convince United Artists to back his film version of the play. Therefore, even if McLure couldn't save it in New York, Altman could bring it to a much wider audience around the country. Altman also wanted Sigourney as the lead in the picture. She would be able to work together with the man she loved. It seemed almost fairy tale.

Unfortunately, United Artists, possibly because of the play's poor showing on Broadway, got cold feet and pulled out. Altman was unable to find anyone else to back it, and the project died. That death spelled the eventual end of Sigourney and McLure's relationship as well.

Because Sigourney didn't have to worry about where the next meal would be coming from (even if she didn't find work), the fact that she was still looking for another good film role a year after her first one didn't seem to panic her as much as it might have affected someone else. As a matter of fact, she finished 1980 by working out the details and getting ready to star in Durang's *Beyond Therapy*. It wasn't Broadway, but it was fun. It would also be a departure from looking at roles intended for bimbos. In the film world, that seemed to be all she (or most actresses, for that matter) was being offered.

Beyond Therapy opened in early January at New York's Phoenix Theater. Besides Sigourney, the cast included Stephen Collins, Kate McGregor-Stewart, and Jim Borrelli. The reviewers loved it, and they particularly liked Sigourney.

The play, as off-the-wall as the usual offerings of Durang-Weaver, centered on two people who become acquainted via a personals ad in a literary magazine. But rather than being a simple story about these two people meeting in a restaurant, their analysts are also included, and the presentation becomes a satirical and hilarious attack on psychiatrists, their jargon, and their work. Presented were two characters who couldn't do anything in life without consulting their shrinks. Sigourney's character, Prudence, brings the house down in the second act when she pulls a gun and demands to order. Rather than call the police, the waiter follows through and the craziness begins again. Durang and Weaver were once again being tabbed as winners.

Sigourney was still wondering if she would get an opportunity to play another strong woman in the movies when Peter Yates offered her the lead in *Eyewitness*. Sensing that the role of television reporter Tony Sokolow was the kind of part she could also play in real life, she immediately took it.

She described her new character this way: "Tony is the daughter of cultured, wealthy parents who defies their expectations and takes a job in a newsroom. But even worse, from their point of view, she falls in love with a Vietnam veteran who works as a janitor and is totally out of place in the elite social world that she and her family belong to. He witnesses a murder that she's investigating, and their romance places both of their lives in jeopardy."

In some ways, Tony was just like Sigourney. She was trying to fit into two different worlds at the same time.

Other actresses would have simply relied on watching the news to prepare for the picture, but not Sigourney. Contacting WNEW-TV in New York, she received permission to become a part of a reporter's team. She wanted to learn firsthand what reporters did and how she could bring this realism to the screen. Such an experience meant a great deal to her.

"I spent three weeks with reporter Aida Alvarez and her crew, covering everything from a drug bust to the Scarsdale doctor murder case. It was very exciting work. I got a sense of the long days a reporter puts in and was exposed to the city in ways my character would never have experienced if she had stayed within the confines of her family's privileged environment." Certainly that was true. Sigourney also covered a story of finding different parts of a man's body in different places around the city. He had evidently mistreated a prostitute and she had taken her pay out of his hide, literally.

While Sigourney was working with Channel 5, she was also taking piano lessons and learning how to ride a horse. Her character Tony did both of these things, and Sigourney wanted to perform them with the grace and style of someone who had always done them.

David Baker taught her piano, and in just two weeks she learned well enough to play Mendelssohn in the film.

When filming started, she felt and acted like a reporter, a horsewoman, and a musician. The crew had never seen anything like it.

Still, as filming opened, Sigourney felt more than a bit unnerved by the world of motion pictures . . . it was so very different from her experiences on stage so far. Even with a film under her belt, she wasn't used to the pace or the manner in which a picture was put together.

In an interview at that time she attempted to relate her fears and the reasons for them, and why producer Peter Yates made these apprehensions subside.

"I'm used to the solid experience of the theater, which gives you breathing time. Movies are crazy. Sometimes you don't even know what you're going to shoot the next day.

"Peter Yates manages to create an atmosphere of trust. He is sensitive to the actors and makes time for them. He never forgets that the story is about people, and doesn't

get carried away with the technical aspects
of the film to the extent of neglecting the
problems of the actors that need solving.

"I love the theater, but I have to say there
is something very exhilarating about films,
apart from the joy of working with great actors, like my idol Irene Worth. It has to do
with the sheer energy of it and with the
hundreds of people who are a apart of it,
making you look good. It's an incredible
amount of work and, like life, it's frustrating
because it keeps going on and you can't get
it back and do it over. You can never play
the scene again."

Of course, thanks to the world of film, Sigourney's last statement was not entirely true.
Not only could you play a scene over again,
but it happens all the time with retakes in
film.

With the likes of Sigourney, William Hurt,
Christopher Plummer, and James Wood, 20th
Century Fox figured that they had a sure
winner in *Eyewitness*. On paper the plot looked
good, too.

William Hurt's character, Daryll Deever, a
night janitor, has two loves. One is his mo-
torcycle, the other a news reporter he watches
every night on his VCR. Daryll witnesses a

murder, and into his life comes the sophisticated reporter, Tony Sokolow, that he has fantasized about. By giving misleading statements, he keeps the story alive, thus prolonging his contact with the reporter. Despite the fact that their characters are badly mismatched, they become involved in a love affair that places their lives in danger.

The movie is a "who dunnit," and it was an attempt by screenwriter Steve Tesich—whose film *Breaking Away* captured the hearts of the world—to bring back the wonderful suspense dramas of Hollywood's Golden Era. It looked like it would work. It seemingly should have gotten a much larger audience than it did.

The movie received quite a lot of press during filming. Critic Rex Reed even tried, unsuccessfully, to obtain a story line for the film. Everyone associated with the film had worked successfully on other projects. Yet when *Eyewitness* opened, it was not a success. The combined talents of all the principals involved simply didn't spell magic.

Reviewers mainly had positive things to say about the film, but the reasons they tended to like it was that it was done with a professional approach, and the actors, director, and producers seemed to mesh the plot very well. (Although if one particular complaint came out of the reviews, it was that the plot lacked reality.)

New York magazine said that Sigourney's performance "had the elongated elegance that makes earnestness chic." Vincent Canby of the *New York Post* liked her acting, too, but he found the film a bit short on reality. As the reviews from across the nation came in, it was obvious that while critics didn't dislike the movie, it wasn't going to be considered a "must see" either. Some reviews showed a bit of disdain as well.

Andrew Sarris, writing in the *Village Voice*, said, "The best that I can say for *Eyewitness* is that I was engrossed to the very end by its half-baked audacity." *The New York Times* used these words: "Logic doesn't score in the movie, but feelings do." But the public's view may have been best seized by Archer Winston in the *New York Post:* "In short, it can't be rated as amounting to much in the long run."

Sigourney had played a role with some meat, but the film hadn't gone over well in middle America. To most of the nation, she was still the girl in the underwear who had beaten the alien. Playing a strong Jewish princess hadn't changed her image. As it was, by the time *Eyewitness* premiered in 1981, Sigourney had already finished another picture and was working on her fourth. *Eyewitness*'s failure must have been a blow to her ego, but it hardly hindered her career and the fact that people still wanted her to star in their films.

Yet, even as she worked on Hollywood films, Sigourney remained a New York girl. She didn't want to give up her life, her friends, or the city she had really always called home, even if it meant having her career suffer a bit as a result. Retaining her independence, she was still more stage oriented than motion-picture oriented.

As *Eyewitness* quickly fled out of the theaters and found its way over to cable, so too did the McLure-Weaver union find its way out the door with the two lovers looking for new interests and partners. Sigourney began 1981 in much the same way she had ended 1979: alone and looking for a good part.

10

After concluding the filming of *Eyewitness*, Sigourney decided to return to the stage. Her status as a major motion-picture personality (if not a bona fide star) had positioned her to finally obtain a major part on Broadway. As 1981 wound down, she prepared for the female lead in Nicol Williamson's production of *Macbeth*. Every trade paper in the country reported her signing, and it was considered significant enough by the general news media to obtain space in weekly journals such as *Newsweek*.

Shakespeare's bloody Scottish play, however, has always had a reputation as a presentation that brings bad luck. This production proved especially true for Sigourney.

Not only was Williamson producing the play, but he was also playing Macbeth. From day one it became obvious that his version of what Lady Macbeth should be and Sigourney's version were very different. As a matter of fact, she had planned on presenting Lady Macbeth as a much more modern woman than Williamson wanted. The niggling battles of interpretation began.

During the first week of January and just ten days before the play was to be previewed, Sigourney quit (later she would admit to being fired). She cited artistic differences with Williamson as her reason. Evidently, the two simply couldn't get together and find any compromises. The end result was a play with two actors seeing the other ruining their concept and presentation. And since the director rarely quits or fires himself, the other party usually leaves. Such was the case with this *Macbeth*.

The New York gossip columns, hot for a story on the always secretive Sigourney, received no real juicy tidbits on the breakup no matter how hard they tried. Williamson wouldn't run her down, the crew said they saw no arguments, and everyone had nothing but praise for how easy it had been to work with the actress. Still, despite this lack of criticism, the move did leave Sigourney with many negative press reports she didn't need. She was unfairly labeled as a quitter in some camps, as headstrong and hard to work with in others. Most devastating, she would miss an outstanding opportunity to play in a leading role on a Broadway stage. It may have been slightly easier to take for Sigourney, however, when the play failed almost as soon as it opened.

Sigourney didn't have to sit around for long, luckily. She was offered and accepted the part of the English born-and-bred lady, Jill Bryant, in the film *Year of Living Dangerously*. The part allowed her to escape from New York and the string of bad luck she had been living through in the city and travel to the other side of the world—the Philippines—for location shooting.

Like her previous role as a reporter in *Eyewitness*, this opportunity looked like the one to push her career beyond that of "the promising actress who starred in *Alien*." She was starring with cinema heartthrob, Australian actor Mel Gibson. MGM was wholeheartedly committed to making this film a box office blockbuster. And the subject matter—passion and romance amid the cultural upheaval and political intrigue in Indonesia in 1965—seemed perfect for a modern American audience.

Gibson played an Australian radio correspondent who loses his eye but gets the girl, Sigourney, amid gunfire, steamy jungle action, and hot tropical nights. It had action, adventure, intrigue, passion, and two beautiful stars. What more could it need?

Maybe what it really needed was better security. For as it turned out, not all of the action took place on the screen. While filming in the Muslim quarter of Manila, over 10,000 Filipinos were crushed into a tiny area. The outraged citizens were wrongly convinced that the movie was anti-Islamic. The crowd squeezed the set, pushed their way by the crew in some cases, and brought the acting to a standstill.

This ugly development was supposedly created when anti-American Iranians spread rumors about the content of the film's script. While unfounded, the rumors did stir up local leaders, who organized the mob. The crowd uttered oaths, and many individuals and different paramilitary groups called in threats to the hotel where the cast and crew were staying.

Sigourney and Mel Gibson were constantly being asked if they were afraid to die or if they lacked courage. As the days crawled by, the crowds grew more and more brazen. Finally, sensing that all hell could literally break loose at any moment, Australian director Peter Weir and producer James McElroy decided to pull out and finish their last eight days of shooting in Australia. The evacuation of cast and crew, over sixty people in all, cost in excess of $120,000, but studio press releases reported that it probably saved many lives.

The decision was made very quickly. At 2:00 P.M. one afternoon Sigourney was told that they would be pulling out. At 2:20 she was told to pack her bags . . . *fast!* At 4:00 she was on a plane headed Down Under.

It was ironic that the Muslims, less than 2 percent of the city's total population, had the power and the organized skills to shut the production down. The only reason that the film was being shot in Manila rather than in

Indonesia, the actual location of the film's story, was that the Indonesian site had been unavailable to fit in with the shooting schedule. Why had the locals gotten so worked up?

Some Australian sources claimed that the near-riots were staged as an attempt to garner advance publicity for the film. They further stated that shooting in the section had been completed, and that it was all an elaborate plot devised by the producer. No one has ever found out the whole truth. In any case, Sigourney was glad to get out. "There were guns everywhere. On every floor of the hotel there was an armed guard," Sigourney told *People Weekly.*

"It wasn't pleasant; it was very difficult. But even now I can say it was the most all-encompassing film experience I've had, probably because we were on the other side of the world, and we were this little group working on this extraordinary story. It was terribly difficult, and terribly inspiring. It was like a rollercoaster . . . but you felt very alive."

While the action and terror of Manila did not thrill the actress, and while the long hours and lack of comforts were not all that pleasing, she obviously loved the story, the people she worked with, and especially the character she played.

"I missed her company for about a year [after filming]. I felt I missed her serenity somehow. It's odd, and I may sound like a crazy person, but I miss not getting to be with her anymore. I have no reason to, I can't bring her back, I can't call her up." Once again Sigourney had become very wound up in a fantasy role.

In many ways *Year* is probably her favorite picture. It was an adventure, the kind she had dreamed of living, and she and the actor she worked with, Mel Gibson, became good friends. Director Peter Weir felt that they could become a hot screen duo. He wanted their love scenes to be very sensual and seductive, but not explicit. He shot them as if they could set a moment of the action ablaze with a mere look or a kiss (especially successful was the scene where Gibson yanks Sigourney out of a stuffy party and kisses her until she's breathless. Many a woman would have loved to have been in Sigourney's shoes for *that* one). To show his stars what he wanted, he had the two watch the love scenes between Cary Grant and Ingrid Bergman in Hitchcock's *Notorious*.

Mel and Sigourney were sizzling and those who saw *Year of Living Dangerously* felt that their chemistry was believable and romantic.

Some younger audiences even felt that it was kind of original. For Sigourney the scenes worked, too, and she couldn't get enough of working with Gibson. "He's a great guy. Someone that good-looking should be so conceited, and he's not at all. He is a very good actor, very funny, very normal, just a regular guy. He's terribly talented. I don't think we've even begun to see what he can do. I'd love to work with him again."

In reality, Sigourney's role in the film didn't really amount to a large number of minutes on screen. She may have been listed as the main star, but Gibson and Linda Hunt dominated the film. Sigourney was the love interest who captured Gibson's attention and with whom he was reunited (a terribly sappy ending) when the film concluded.

Meanwhile, Hunt's role as a male dwarf was a fascinating study in acting. She became a he, and her talent, unusual looks, and mannerisms—as well as the pain and anguish often written on her face—were what captured the critics' and moviegoers' imaginations. She would win an academy award— the first ever for a woman impersonating a man—while the two more famous stars would win little applause at all.

One interesting thing happened during the filming of a scene set around a pool. Sigourney's character came out of the water, immediately grabbing Gibson's attention. They meet, they chat, and the audience of course believes that it was a very warm summer's day. Actually, the weather was freezing, and the actors, especially the very wet Sigourney, were putting on the performances of their lives.

When the film was released, the reviews were mixed but basically pretty good. Some critics thought that it was one of the year's best films, galvanized, especially, by Linda Hunt's astonishing performance. *Time* applauded the effort, and Michael Sragow of *Rolling Stone* went so far as to say that the film "is ambitious and compelling; one of the few movies to capture, with any complexity, the supreme bafflement and terror of Western man confronting the squalor of a depressed and volatile Eastern civilization." Yet for all of this high praise, *Newsweek* answered like this: "It is an annoying failure because it fritters away so many rich opportunities." Still others weren't impressed at all. But once again the good reviews and the chemistry between the starring players didn't

spell big box office success. The film did little
to help stretch Sigourney's image with the
public because so few ended up seeing it. In
many of their minds, she was, *still*, the girl
in *Alien*, fighting the monster in her underwear. In the words of Richard Corliss of *Time*,
"Someday Hollywood will figure out how to
make [Sigourney] a star."

Undoubtedly, to fickle Hollywood, the image of failure began to try to attach itself to
Sigourney Weaver. She could shrug it off, but
the question was, Would other film directors?

Coming out of filming, Sigourney returned
to New York and immediately went back to
her roots. She began looking for a play in
which she could feel the warmth of a theater
and a live audience. She found the perfect
role in the Berkshire Theater Festival in
Stockbridge, Massachusetts.

She was cast as Anne Twomey in Phillip
Barry's 1932 comedy of manners, *The Animal Kingdom*. She earned a whopping $311.75
a week, but she loved the work, even wondering why she got paid at all. "It was so
much fun!" she claimed. Perhaps as much as
anything she was enjoying not working under the gun. She was freed from the pressures of making a hit. On a movie set or a

Broadway stage, those pressures were very real.

Still, Hollywood wanted to know if she could truly do something that would turn out to be the perfect showcase of not only her talent and potential but a megahit as well. Producers were getting tired of her turning down what they thought were good roles to take others that seemed to lead nowhere. The fact that critics had liked her in *Eyewitness* didn't impress the public.

The movers and shakers in the motion-picture world wanted to see the girl get some drive and ambition. Actually, they wanted to see her get a little hungry, to *need* them and their junk roles. But hungry was something this actress had never been. She didn't act or pick parts because she wanted to make big bucks or buy a new car or condo or see her face on *People* magazine. She did it because she wanted to.

Another real problem that the powers-that-be in the Hollywood movie industry were having with her lifestyle was the way she hated publicity and fame. She didn't want to hit the talk shows, she didn't want to be interviewed all the time, and she didn't want to be recognized on the street, go to all the in clubs, or sign autographs. She couldn't be considered a serious star (by their standards) without playing the game—and she wasn't going to play the game. This was considered a real detriment to the success of her pictures. Who wants to pay five bucks to see a movie star who doesn't get her name in the papers and her picture on the cover of magazines? Sigourney didn't have a public or a private image and didn't want one. She was simply too independent.

Film stars may not want to see their photographs on covers of supermarket tabloids, but the studios do. The public had cared about Ripley, but they hadn't cared very much for Sigourney's next two characters.

By mid-1982, Sigourney had proven that she could act. She had not proven that she knew how to choose the right part, to deliver the right kind of off-screen image, and grow into the kind of actress that the American public wanted to see. She was good, but she wasn't box office. Her success didn't seem to be assured—but then again, she didn't seem to care.

11

Sigourney left summer stock, spent time in New York going to the theater and visiting friends, and then went to work on another film. Like her previous ventures, this one called for her to be a completely different character than she had previously portrayed. Also like the others, this one should have had the makings of a real hit.

The movie starred *Saturday Night Live* alumnus Chevy Chase. Needless to say, it was a comedy, a very black comedy. Its subject matter—arms sales—was unusual for this genre. And once again, staid and stodgy Hollywood producers would wonder why Sigourney would have turned down countless parts they considered solid in films of a serious nature for one calling for her to be anything but serious. It also contained little, if any, redeeming social value.

In a way the two stars of *Deal of the Century*, Chase and Weaver, had a similar problem. Both had come on the scene quickly, been called brilliant, and then after initial success, struggled in films that didn't capture the public's fancy. In most cases, reviewers had loved them, but questioned their choice of films.

In public, the two stars were very different. No one had to beg Chase to go on a talk show or play the Hollywood star. He shone brightest when he was in the public eye. His quick wit, slapstick style of pratfalls, and warm, even slightly silly smile were often seen in magazines, newspapers, and on the tube. He was not a real risk. He would do his part to attempt to sell a project.

Sigourney, of course, possessed many of the same characteristics as her costar. She was quick of wit and wonderful to interview.

Unfortunately, she didn't like being a star, and in many ways was her own worst enemy because she rarely promoted her projects. She was not a nurturer. She gave birth to a part and then looked for something else to catch her attention and challenge her imagination. Most of all, she considered herself far too serious of an actress to play Hollywood games.

She said during several interviews given during the filming of *Deal of the Century:* "I've always thought of myself as an actor, not an actress. The word 'actor' seems to mean craft while the word 'actress' tends to translate into feather boas."

Yet feather boas and public appearances sold tickets in the motion picture game. The source of why her image didn't correspond and sell with normal America is easy to recognize.

Sigourney Weaver had never been a part of normal America. Unlike other stars such as Dolly Parton or Burt Reynolds, who knew that people wanted to see them enjoying the same things as anyone else, Sigourney had no real concept as to why this contact was important. She simply hadn't been there. Her mentality didn't mesh with that of the real population, and *that* population bought most of the tickets to movies in which she was appearing. More often than not, middle America went to see a movie to see a *star*, not a story.

Of course she did understand the New York theater audience. They were more sophisticated, and cared less as to who was in a vehicle as to where it was playing, who had written it and was producing it, and what the subject matter was. To them, the theater was more than two hours of escapism—it was a social event. It meant fine clothes, fine atmosphere, and, to a certain extent, rubbing elbows with others who were like you. More often than not, Broadway or off-Broadway wouldn't play in Peoria, or for that matter even in Hollywood.

The two worlds were very different, and rarely did they mix. Most serious Broadway actors never made very much of a splash in the world of motion pictures. If anything, it was much easier to go the other way, because a star was a star, and if that star could really act, then that star would find success in a good Broadway show.

Even today, Sigourney doesn't find the prospect of being famous or sought-after too appealing. "I don't think any of it matters. I don't know why anyone would really want it. Who wants to be recognized by people on the street? Luckily, in New York no one really cares."

So, Warner Brothers had a problem. They wanted Ms. Weaver and her considerable talents in the film, but they knew that she wasn't going to be interested in much more than doing a great job and going home. She was, in her own words, "a New York actress."

To fully explain what that means is to explain why many Hollywood producers who once would have given anything for her were still shying away. They knew she would throw herself into a role and give the best she could, with no prima donna demands. In *Eyewitness* she went out with a television crew and learned how to report; in *Alien*, she studied long and hard to discover all the facets of why her character would react in the manner she did; and in *Year of Living Dangerously*, she studied and knew the history of the events they were filming almost better than the writers. But when a film wrapped, she was ready to move on. Six months of promotions did not suit her.

In New York, when a curtain drops you are

through until the next night. If a play closes, it closes—the actors move on. While the show is going, they give their all to the parts, and they let the publicity people do the rest. Sigourney pulled no punches; this was what acting was about for her.

The press kit for *Deal of the Century* indicated that the producers knew just what they could expect from their star. One passage read, "The actress prides herself on her acting craft and shuns the trappings of celebrity." If Warner Brothers had known how the critics and moviegoing public were going to respond to their film, they might have shunned it, too.

The premise seemed funny. Chase, playing Eddie Muntz, seemed to have all the necessary quirks to make a sublimely self-centered, greedy, immoral arms salesman. He could deadpan his way through scenes with third-world dictators and fall through demonstrations of secondhand arms. Chase would say before the release of the film, "The world of arms sales is so frightening, you have no choice but to laugh. If you don't, most likely you'll go build a bomb shelter."

Screenwriter Paul Brickman had scored with *Risky Business*, had labored four years with this script, and believed he had a hit of the same proportions as his former huge success. Yet what he had thought would bring laughs failed to bring smiles.

Others trapped in the failure were the mul-titalented Gregory Hines, veteran actor Vince Edwards, and of course, Sigourney. She played a rich and ambitious widow whose husband had once sold weapons. To make a huge sale, she would stoop so low as to sleep with a dictator of a sixth-rate third-world country.

The movie was shot at various outdoor lo-cations around southern California and in the soundstages of Burbank Studios. It should have been shot on the set of *Saturday Night Live,* for it didn't deserve much more than a short spot on the late-night show. There, it might have been funny.

The reviews that came out were terrible, and more critics probably saw the film than paying customers. *Variety* stated it best this way: "*Century* is one of those annoying films where the most bizarre things will happen in one scene, and then never be mentioned again. Given everything else, however, that's prob-ably a blessing." *The New York Times* pointed out the film's problem in a very blunt fashion: "It's terrible." With a plot centered on the

selling of bombs, America would not go for
it.

Sigourney had hoped that the role would
prove that she could do comedy. It didn't. As
a matter of record, about the nicest thing any
reviewer said about her performance was that
she was attractive.

Alien was now ancient history. It had been
her one hit. Her other films had not scored
well at the box office, and with each new role
reviewers who had once loved her now
seemed more and more likely to roast her.
She was headed down a street where many
overnight sensations often stall: trivialand.

However, secure in the fact that she was
an actress, that she did have brains, and that
even if she bombed she was doing what she
wanted, the state of her film career still
seemed to matter little to her. She was much
more concerned with making sure that she
found roles that would let her expand and
grow. As long as she felt good about herself,
the public's perception wasn't as important
as some would like to think.

Back in New York she settled into her comfortable apartment and began to catch up on
the local theater scene. She also took time
off to return to Williamstown, Massachusetts

for a few weeks of summer stock. There she was directed by a young Californian named John Simpson.

The play, *Old Times,* earned great reviews, and the actress felt comfortable once more on the planks of a stage. She was back in a medium she loved and understood. It was a place where all that was required was talent, and Sigourney gave all she had. At night it was good wine and new friends. And the immediate feedback was also better than having to wait a year to find out what the rest of the world thought of you and your film.

Still, even during these calm times, there was a restlessness about Sigourney. She had a great deal more that she felt she needed to accomplish, other parts she wanted to play, and a talent she felt was not being properly used. There had to be something out there that wouldn't bore her.

"I like change," she said. "I like to have a job that changes constantly, and since I've never been able to make up my mind what I wanted to do with my life, acting gives me a chance to try out all these things. I keep thinking that someday I'll play a role, and I'll like the role so much that I'll end up going back to school and becoming a lawyer or a biologist."

As she had in the past, she sought the change she needed and continued her search for a suitable role. As had also often happened in the past, she was told by producers and casting consultants that she was a wonderful actress, but with her background and education she just wasn't the small-town Texas waitress type.

Rather than take this as a definitive answer, she would often use her own money to fly to a producer and attempt to get a chance to audition. She used this tactic to fly to England to see Fred Zinneman and attempt to have him cast her in *Five Days of Summer*, but he felt she wasn't right for the part of a woman who would cavort around the Alps. Undaunted, she went to bat for herself whenever she found a part she thought was meaty, even while realizing that her stereotyping wouldn't have put her on the consideration list for the role.

Once again she was hearing many of the same old lines: You're too tall, too beautiful, too dignified. Added to this list was: You're far too well-schooled for what we want. How frustrating it must have been to hear that if you'd been trained to act at a great school, it meant you were too well-trained to play the role of a normal person. In a sense, Sigourney had become a poor little rich girl.

Still, she couldn't suddenly become poor and relive her life. Nothing was going to make her give up who she was and what she loved. She wasn't going to jam with Mick Jagger or join Roy Acuff at the Grand Ole Opry simply to prove she was one of the people. By the same token, she wasn't really the type to publicly identify herself with charities or causes merely to change middle America's view of her. The only way for her image to change was through a perfect role. And it didn't take a genius to tell her that if she didn't find that part soon, it might be too late.

12

Sigourney had always used her own best judgment in choosing parts, and then had given her best when she was awarded those parts. Yet the fact that she had won a Drama Desk award didn't matter. It had become apparent that she had been given a rare shot at the big time and was not doing very much with it. She had been so selective in her roles that she had almost taken herself out of the business. She still needed a hit. As 1983 wound to a close, two things happened to change her career and her life.

While it was true that she didn't want to play rich society girls or educated and cultured women all of her life, she now wanted to act more than she wanted to be picky. But even so, she simply couldn't do a part just because it was offered to her.

"I think sometimes if you're in a film that you don't really love, I think my work would suffer. After a certain number of films, I do think it's getting easier for me and I'm getting a lot less serious about all of this. So maybe someday I'll just do it 'for the money.'" But she wasn't going to do that quite yet.

For a young actress who had traveled all over the world trying to talk people into giving her roles yet had often turned down a chance at so many others offered to her, the next part she accepted may have shocked a great many film insiders. Serious acting it wasn't, but the uniquely humorous aspect of Sigourney's personality may have been behind the reason she took the role. She freely admitted that she loves to prove people wrong and do exactly the opposite of what they expect. During her interview with director Ivan Reitman for a role in his "ghost" movie, she said, "Oh Ivan, multiple schizophrenics are my specialty."

Ghostbusters seemed to be another studio risk, but this time the powers-that-be weren't really pulling on Sigourney's name or acting ability to ring the cash registers. Far from it—the part she won was very small. Still, she was involved in something that would provide the most fun she'd ever had on a motion picture set.

"It was fun. I loved being the demon; that was my favorite part, I must say. I loved levitating, and I loved turning into a dog. I loved all those things because you see, that's the kind of thing you usually do on stage. You usually don't get to do that; you don't have a split-personality movie. God forbid, a woman with a split personality. She might do something unsympathetic! But you see, here I could do it and it was funny."

When originally describing her role she told the press, "I play a character who has a problem with a major appliance in my home—it's possessed. The film's premise is that this is a common household problem. This is not something on a television special. Everyone in the city has a ghost problem and it's getting out of hand. There is only one group who can take care of it—the Ghostbusters."

She was joined in the film by Bill Murray,

Dan Aykroyd, and Harold Ramis, so it marked her second straight attempt at comedy and working with talented comics (Murray and Aykroyd) whose first public recognition came from *Saturday Night Live.*

The movie was a refreshing change of pace for the actress. She was working with people who were as crazy and off-the-wall in real life as she was. From day one she knew she had made a great choice. "I knew the work would be loose, crazy, and spontaneous. The guys were all very generous. There was no ego on this show. It was all very giving, which was wonderful."

Not only was her role as Dana Barrett a great deal of fun, but it allowed her to come into the set every week or two and then take ten days off. The pressure, the crazy grind of fifteen-hour days on the set, wasn't a part of her life this time. Her role was important, even essential, but it wasn't so time-consuming that it took her away from the things she really loved to do. It was like working part-time.

Everyone who had been associated with *Deal of the Century, Eyewitness,* and *Year of Living Dangerously* had been convinced that the combination of actors, writers, directors, and plots would signal a major bonanza at the box office. In all honesty, the people on the *Ghostbusters* set were not as cocky. They believed all the elements were there, but they wondered if what they were selling would play to a baby-boomer crowd.

The plot was unique but not original in concept. Bob Hope and Paulette Goddard had cleaned up ghosts some forty years before in a film called *Ghostbreakers.* Abbott and Costello had done it on many occasions in their careers. But this movie would combine new comic talents, a crazy and laidback sense of humor with amazing special effects, hopefully creating enough laughs for people to buy the premise of New York being taken over by spirits.

Dan Aykroyd was responsible for the original script. A card-carrying member of the American Society for Psychical Research, he felt it was a sure bet to work with the American audience of the mid-1980s. He put it this way at an early press conference: "We're just doing the modern version of the old-time ghost movies. The only difference is that we have a little more technology than our predecessors."

Production actually began in October of

1983 in New York. Locations included the New York Public Library on Fifth Avenue, City Hall, Columbia University, Central Park, and the old New York Police Department lockup. For Sigourney, it meant she could continue to live in her own apartment while the actors and crew from the West Coast had to make do in new digs.

The second half of the film was shot in Burbank and Los Angeles. The entire project wrapped just four months after shooting began. For Sigourney, less than a month of her time had been spent playing Dana Barrett.

Dana, a classical musician, was not unlike Sigourney. She loved culture, her privacy, and was comfortable in her own company. She also liked spontaneous people. But for the first time, the role would show Sigourney still living in a modest apartment, working a normal job, possessing normal ambitions and a normal wardrobe. In essence she would be someone with whom everyone could relate, playing a role in which the public could like her again. Perhaps she even had something to give her some identity other than that of an alien killer.

The major disappointment to Sigourney was not being able to turn into a dog via the use of makeup and special effects. She loved the thought of playing the mad, moaning animal. Even without this portrayal, she had convinced almost every man on the set that she was one of the sexiest numbers with whom they had ever worked.

When the filming was over, she was almost sad. Almost three years later she would still miss the moments and people associated with the film. "I missed the boys after *Ghostbusters*, and I kept looking around for those three guys! It seemed so lonely not to have all three of them there, somehow. And I haven't seen the three of them together since we stopped, which is too bad."

The most important verdict associated with the film hadn't come in yet. The crew had had a blast, the actors had worked well together, and things had come out of production without a hitch. But what would the reviewers and the public think? The cast and crew would have to wait about four months to find out.

During the summer of 1984, *Ghostbusters* became a smash hit, and it would prove to be the one to put Sigourney Weaver back in the public eye in a major way. Janet Maslin of *The New York Times* would say, "Miss

Weaver looks great and shows herself to be a willing comedienne." David Ansen of *Newsweek* was equally complimentary. As he wrote: "After being mauled by director William Friedkin in *Deal of the Century*, [she] gets to show what a fine and sexy comedienne she can be." Reviewer after reviewer loved her scenes, calling her talented, sexy, witty, and a fine actress. For the first time since her initial film, the critics seem bedazzled by her once again.

Even more importantly, the movie was heralded as a fun flick, perhaps the first movie of its genre to succeed in making the absurd plausible since the work of W.C. Fields. *Ghostbusters* was a huge step above *CaddyShack*, another Murray vehicle, and it appealed to a much wider audience than *Blues Brothers*, a previous Aykroyd success (with the late John Belushi). And most important for Sigourney, audiences in Dubuque and Waco would not only turn out to see it, but they would find themselves fascinated and entertained by the actress. On a wide scale, this was a first for her.

In *Alien* the plot and technical ploys had seduced the audience, and the actors merely served to move the plot along; they were objects upon which viewers could project their own terror. In Sigourney's other three films, the public hadn't turned out in large enough numbers to make up its collective mind about her. But in *Ghostbusters,* she finally became more than a prop or an actress in an overlooked film—she was a real person.

Suddenly, staring out from the front of magazines and newspapers was a photograph of Sigourney in a sexy red dress, a seductive growl on her face, legs looking impossibly long and shapely and tousled hair literally flowing down her neck and back. She had successfully turned America on. Ironically, except for the usual publicity-type release hype and the occasional interview, she refused to play the Hollywood Star game. She had arrived—and could still play by her own rules.

After the movie she returned to New York. She'd had enough of Hollywood to know that the movie business was insanity, and there were very few people crazy enough to be able to enjoy it for what it was. In *Ghostbusters* she had found just those kind of people and they had made the shoot almost as enjoyable as performing in the theater. Yet even this rush of excitement wasn't enough to make her change. Far from it. Sigourney was much more interested in finding a good play and someone to direct her in it.

What she found was David Rabe's *Hurlyburly*, a scorching behind-the-scenes glimpse at the Hollywood male. Sigourney's role as a mistress—hardly the kind of lifestyle the self-assured Sigourney would tolerate—offered her a wonderful opportunity to stretch her talent and her image. After several false starts, *Hurlyburly* would find her attempting another Broadway production. She could set her sights on just acting, in the place she'd trained to be in so many years before. One role, each night, before a different audience, with actors and crew honing and sharpening their skills to approach perfection. This was why she loved doing what she did, and here was a wonderful vehicle to show the world just what she was . . . an actor.

The play was made much more enjoyable because one of her favorite leading men, and former *Eyewitness* costar, William Hurt, was joining her. Another skilled actor who was put off by the games Hollywood wanted its stars to play, Hurt (like Sigourney) was a rebel with real acting as his cause. He wanted to be known by and judged on his craft, not his life. (He later received the Oscar for best actor for his performance in *Kiss of the Spider Woman.*)

When speaking of Hurt, Sigourney's eyes usually glow. "You know the more you work with someone, the more you trust each other. Certainly after *Eyewitness* and *Hurlyburly* I'd basically do anything with Bill because it's fun to work with him. I think he's a great actor, unpredictable, and we're good friends, so I think it's a very good chemistry.

"He takes his work very seriously. He searches a lot, which is good, and very inspiring. Most of the time, I feel like I'm too complicated as an actor; he makes me feel very simple because he's on so many levels, it's unbelievable! I'd love to do some Shakespeare with him, and I'd love to do another film with him."

Even more thrilling than the opportunity to work with Hurt was that in *Hurlyburly* Sigourney had finally found a part to completely challenge her. She played a photographer named Darlene. In all honesty, the fact that she didn't look like a Darlene may have shown just that much more of her talent. Her key line—"Everything is always distracting me from everything else"—might well have been the theme to both her own life and that of her father's. Ultimately, playing a mistress and a confused product of the West Coast seemed to bring out the best in the actress.

"The experience itself was so overwhelming, just to be in it, to play a person in that role. It was one of those plays where you thought you could work on it forever. I think Bill and I played each of our two scenes as many different ways as you could, which was fun, because you have to keep finding out things on stage. You really need another partner who you can rely on totally and you know they're not going to go on some bizarre tangent. It made me want to do a real comedy with Bill because our second scene was comic and very funny. I felt we were a funny couple."

The chemistry that so fascinated Sigourney charmed audiences and critics, too. Even though *Hurlyburly* was a Broadway play, it was reviewed from coast to coast. Jack Kroll in *Newsweek* wrote quite a lot about it, mainly offering high praise for everyone associated with the project. About the ensemble of actors (Hurt, Weaver, Jerry Stiller, Cynthia Nixon, Christopher Walken, Judith Ivey, and

Harvey Keitel) he said, "They are all superb." About Sigourney he stated, "Weaver's razor-edged beauty and haute-couture vulnerability" made her excellent in the role. The critic went on to conclude, "The play, on or off-Broadway, is going to be seen all over America for a long time to come."

Others loved it and thought it as important as *Newsweek* had. Richard Schickel would write in *Time*, "Theirs [the whole cast and crew] is an important work, masterfully accomplished." Frank Rich, writing for *The New York Times*, didn't find it as satisfying as most others, but even he was impressed with the group of people who played out the roles on the stage. "It seems too good to be true," he wrote, "to walk into an off-Broadway theater and find a half-dozen of our best young actors performing a new David Rabe play under the directions of Mike Nichols."

When Broadway's Tony Award nominations were announced, Sigourney's name was called. Now the world knew that she was a real actress. After all, it had taken a great deal of effort and talent to stand out among the group of individuals she had worked with in this production. She must have felt as though she had reached the point she had always wanted to reach, and was now considered by her peers and the world to be a serious actress. It was ironic that she had earned this respect due to a play mocking the Hollywood system she'd never wanted to be a part of her life.

Sigourney had gone from becoming a near-washout in movies to (once again) Hollywood's newest sexy star; from being all-but-forgotten in the New York theater to being one of Broadway's actresses; and from not having very many fans who cared much about her to having a legion of Americans wanting to know when they could see her again. For the second time in her career, she was hot. *Harpers Bazaar* magazine labeled her one of the most beautiful women in America. To prove the point, she posed for them in a black, low-cut Valentino sheath, revealing moles and a bit more besides (proving she had more than just a great set of legs!). She revealed in the interview accompanying the photograph that she loved video games and ice cream. The unapproachable rich girl was becoming an accessible woman, one a man (or a fan) might be able to touch. No longer was she seen as the rich bitch she had once seemed to be.

Not surprisingly, the press and the hype following her two hits, the "great" roles in films and plays now being pitched her way, the awards that might soon be hers—none of these interested her much. As a matter of fact, during the same period when her career was taking her up to the top, something far more important was beginning to take her far higher in her private life. Sigourney was falling in love.

13

It began in earnest in October of 1983 at a Halloween party Sigourney threw at her apartment, but the roots of what was about to spring forth dated back to summer stock in New England.

For three summers, beginning in 1981, Sigourney had appeared in summer theater festivals in Williamstown, Massachusetts. She had loved the experience of acting in front of small audiences in more casual settings than the New York stage. With an inherent openness that allowed for great creativity, the summer-stock productions had, for Sigourney, much the same happy feeling of some of the shows of her Stanford days. More than anything else summer stock had given her a chance to play a variety of roles that she would never play in the regular theater, and that kind of acting was nothing if not fun. It brought out the best in her, so she came back summer after summer to renew herself and her love of her craft.

Each season she was there, she saw and occasionally worked with a Hawaiian-born director named John Simpson. Though six years her junior, he seemed to have a great deal in common with Sigourney. He had been raised in the world of show business, even though his was a totally different perspective and situation than she had seen as the child of a network executive. As a child actor, he had appeared in numerous television shows and movies. By the time he turned seventeen he was pulling down $2,000 a week on the TV series *Hawaii Five-O*. Still, his plans were more ambitious than acting on television, so he left his idyllic world in paradise, trading a life many kids would only dream about for four tough years at Boston University.

While at B.U. he earned high marks for creativity and studied hard enough to receive acceptance to the Yale School of Drama. He, unlike Sigourney, had enjoyed his graduate work and impressed a great number of his peers and teachers. Simpson had an abundance of talent, and he decided he would channel that talent into directing.

By the early eighties he was in Williamstown plying his craft. Though young, he was respected by the well-known actors coming in for the plays as someone who would wisely use his gifts. He had the reputation as someone who was flexible and liked to listen to actors' suggestions about their roles. Most of all, he was no dictator and he didn't consider himself God's gift to the stage.

In addition to Williamstown, he worked at Joseph Papp's Public Theater and the Ensemble Studio Theater in New York. Though not a household name, even among those who knew the world of plays and playwrights, he was fast becoming someone who had the talent and the experience to be reckoned with in the future. Those who had seen his work seemed to think he had the proper techniques and personality to work with just about anyone, including upcoming stars.

Sigourney was one of these up-and-comers. They first worked together in the play *Old Times*. But it would be another three years before the two would actually look at each other in anything but a professional manner.

Sigourney had remembered the director while making out the guest list for her Halloween party. A party at this time of year seemed appropriate, given the nature of her upcoming role in *Ghostbusters*. Simpson, a very private person like the actress, did not immediately respond. But when some of Sigourney's friends worked on him, he finally decided to attend.

No one really remembers if the party was much of a success (it probably was; Sigourney had a reputation for throwing great parties), but the actress and the director did finally sit down and begin to talk. Handsome and assured, he had that air women usually love and men usually admire. When he walked into a room, he owned it. Still, the more he and his host talked, the more Sigourney found herself being drawn to his intelligence, wit, and knowledge of the theater.

Simpson also had to be impressed. He could have his pick of actresses for escorts, and beauty was something he saw so much that he almost took it for granted. So this woman's good looks and acting experience shouldn't have impressed him a great deal, but what did impress him was her mind. Unlike other actresses who were obsessed with stardom or winning awards, she was interested in her craft. She loved the theater, and she wanted to understand, study, and work in all facets of it.

The two spent most of their evening talking, and before the party ended, Sigourney, taking the lead once again, asked John back for an evening of wine and discussion about the theater. Certainly she should have been able to knowledgeably discuss the current crop of plays in New York. (She often went to the theater three times a week when she wasn't working.)

Having both graduated from the Yale School of Drama was another aspect of their lives that brought out mutual stories about classes, professors, experiences, hardships, and the idealistic nature of a student reshaped into the realistic nature of a graduate. The experience of those days—though they went through them during different years—seemed to bring them even closer.

Finally, because Sigourney had not allowed herself to be limited in a role as just an "actress," because she had won some degree of respect as a writer, and because she did find every part of the theater exciting, the totality of their craft and love for it brought Sigourney and John together on a different plane than other relationships had. As a matter of fact, with so much in common they almost belonged to a fraternity with just two members.

Soon, when he wasn't directing and she wasn't acting, they were seen everywhere together. No matter when or where they happened to be, they were communicating. Within months it had become obvious to all who knew them well that their affair would be a long-term one.

Secretive Sigourney at first maintained her tradition of not talking about her personal life. She managed to stay out of society columns, too. But soon, the rush that she now knew was real love was too much for her, and she began to hint in interviews with reporters that she just might be falling head over heels.

As 1984 moved on, she became bolder about talking about how wonderful Mr. Simpson was. For the very first time in her life, she seemed to want strangers to know something about her life outside of the business.

In the past she had peppered her interviews with things like, "I wish people would realize that I'm not too well-educated to play a certain part." Now, she was saying things like, "You haven't asked me about my love life!" For reporters it was a dramatic change.

The Simpson/Weaver courtship went on for a year. It regularly included evenings at the theater, an occasional movie (Sigourney didn't enjoy films very much), nice dinners, and of course a lot of talk. It also included a great camping trip to the director's native Hawaii. Above all, it was spontaneous. Sigourney joked to reporters that they were busy not planning a wedding.

Long after the two had begun to unofficially live with each other, they decided to make it official. Sigourney announced in late summer that they would be married in the fall. She then told the cast of *Hurlyburly* that she would be leaving the show in October. Finally, a very untraditional service was planned for a beautiful late fall day at Pat Weaver's Long Island yacht club.

The invited guests were given wash-off tatoos as favors. They were also encouraged to wear them, and many of them did.

Two ministers were asked to jointly perform the ceremony. Just like the bride and groom, one of the clergy represented a man, the other a woman.

Music was also a bit untraditional. Rather than the usual piano, harp, or organ accompaniment, Sigourney had found a great bongo player and teamed him with a master of the bagpipes.

As guest Bill Murray observed, "It was great fun. But then I've never seen Sigourney give a bad party." To other more stodgy guests, the observation of all the less-than-subtle silliness led them to question whether a serious union would result. But those who knew how unconventional the director and the actress he was marrying were enjoyed themselves and decided this was all a good sign of a fun marriage. In Simpson, they figured, Sigourney had finally found her match.

While they were both very similar, they opened up new doors and directions for each other, too. Perhaps the most important door that John kept opening for his new wife was a constant involvement in what was happening in the theater. She would later admit in an interview with Leslie Bennetts of *The New York Times* wire service that he had "brought her back into a world I might have been stepping out of now." By that she meant that he kept her in touch with plays and live acting. As she began to do more and more films, and particularly since *Ghostbusters* had been such a big boost for her career, she could easily have lost this important facet of her life.

In later interviews, after she'd had an opportunity to look back at her marriage and how it had allowed her to grow, she began to talk about the teamwork and the maturity that John had brought to her life. Rather than a typical show business marriage that often took a backseat to glamour and career, their initial years together seemed to prove that this marriage was based on something a great deal more substantial—communication and need.

Sigourney has freely admitted to loving marriage; not only the act, but the fact that two people are sharing a life and a dream.

"I think it's great. We'd like to work together very much. I think it would be fun. I don't think it would be any big deal. I mean, I think we want to find the right thing, but I feel like I already have worked with my husband, because we're always working around each other and discussing things.

"That's one of the nice things about marrying someone in the same business. He also makes me see how hard it is to be a good director. Why, there are so few good directors around, and I really find his commitment very inspiring. And that, I think, has made a great contribution to my work attitude. It has just enriched it enormously."

Unlike many unions of people in the same business, this one appears to be without jealousy or major conflicts. Possibly the main reason is that both parties have such tremendous self-confidence.

"I don't feel there's any real conflict there [between professional and personal life]. We don't have any children at this point, so I don't feel we've had to choose."

Still, Sigourney's need for John's companionship was shown when she began to talk about being separated because of their work. In a way, the long-time independent lady became a little less self-assured when talking about stays of more than just a few days away from her husband.

"A few months is too long. A few weeks, maybe. But I think one of the things we realize . . . if we had to be apart a few months, it's not worth it. We can do it, and we might do it, but in general it's just not as much fun— the work isn't as much fun if it means you cannot see the person for two months; that's a drag no matter how you look at it. So I think even if we had to be in Africa or New Zealand for six months, we would make sure we could find a way to see each other somehow. We would build it into whatever job we had. Your life is more important than your work, and if you realize that you're giving up your life, then I think your work suffers, and you suffer, and it just doesn't seem to make any sense."

Falling in love coupled with having a successful role in a blockbuster film had begun to push the actress into a favorable place in the average fan's heart. Her interviews still centered around her work, and they didn't dwell on her private life, but she was at least beginning to look more like a person anyone could easily relate to. She was still independent, but a little more mellow. As matter of fact, even as Hollywood called with wonderful opportunities to act in the kind of roles she'd always held out for, Sigourney was telling reporters, "I always never want to get away from home."

Sigourney was truly in love.

14

Sigourney had little time to enjoy her wedded bliss. Because of her success in *Ghostbusters* (and to a lesser extent, *Hurlyburly*) she was in demand by producers, directors, and bankrollers of film projects. She was also, for the very first time, seemingly ready to jump in and work on a full-time basis. Leaving New York was hard on her, but she hungered for acknowledgment and success like she never had before. This hunger excited the film establishment.

Signaling the beginning of the very busy year of 1985, she first packed her bags and flew to England to work with Michael Caine in a British film directed by an American, Bob Swaim, and financed by RKO. Husband John Simpson also made the trip with her, so it could be considered a bit of a working honeymoon for the couple.

Half Moon Street, based on the novel *Doctor Slaughter* by Paul Theroux, was a real breakthrough for the actress. For the very first time in her career, she would have the opportunity to play a woman of the eighties in a leading role, a woman who was complicated, intelligent, witty, and beautiful. Upon reading the script, Sigourney knew that Dr. Lauren Slaughter was someone she could like a great deal. She even said at the time, "Lauren is certainly the best woman character I've ever read. She's certainly the most original. The most intelligent. Usually they are either intelligent or sexual. Sexual and stupid."

In brief, Lauren was a beautiful, smart young graduate student in London who decides to supplement her income by offering her services to an escort agency. In doing this, she begins to move into the world of high finance, politics, and power. She falls in love with a client, a British diplomat played by Michael Caine, and soon is involved in a world of mystery, intrigue, and danger.

The film was director Swaim's from beginning to end. Young, driven, and very creative, he had received the French *César* award—the equivalent of an Oscar—for his debut as a director with *La Nuit des Saint-Germain des Près* in 1977. His style of direction was precise and to a certain degree, dictatorial. But even knowing how he worked didn't keep Sigourney from wanting this "wonderful" part. Nor did the nude scenes or the erotic nature of her character's moonlighting venture. Once again, it was a chance for her to shock a few people, and she always took advantage of that.

Unfortunately, the film received more play in Europe than it did in the States, and it probably will not be viewed by large numbers of Americans until it airs on cable. The reviews that came out were anything but encouraging, but it was fascinating work for the actress. She had no hesitation in talking about what went into the film, her admiration for the people with whom she worked, and her time spent in England. Yet the character of Lauren, the way she changed, the way she grew, why she did what she did, and how it affected her mind was why Sigourney took the role (and why it still means so much to her). Sigourney, unlike may actresses would, spoke of Dr. Lauren Slaughter almost as if she were real, and then, in an almost apologetic manner, attempted to explain and justify Lauren's actions.

"My character has various reasons for doing what she does, but the prime one is just practicality; I just need to make some money fast, I'm good at it, and I get the job. The film doesn't really study what I do as much as how I change. People who want to see me play a call girl are going to be disappointed because what I really do is play a character who decides, I can either take on this extra job nights or I can become a call girl. Well, I guess I'll just become a call girl."

Explaining Lauren's motivation might also signal an attempt by Sigourney to explain why she took the part, and why she enjoyed it so much. For those who found certain things lacking in her portrayal, her words also seem to rationalize why that may be so, too!

"It is not a shock [what her character chooses to do], although I think I enjoy shocking people. It's about what happens when a supremely confident person finds out that she's sort of like everybody else. Not vulnerable, but that she has to pay prices, she can't just do all the things that aren't done and not suffer. She'd never thought she'd have to do that. She thought like a lot of people, well I'm different, I can do it my way and I won't have to bow to the rules of society."

The awakening of Lauren—and why Sigourney was fascinated with her—may be revealed in those last words. The New York actress was beginning to realize that not every game was going to be one in which she could decide just how to do what she wanted to do. The more that she worked in the film business, the more she was learning that she would have to do a few things the way other people wanted her to, because she was only one cog in the filmmaking machine. Acting, the career she had chosen and wanted to do well, was more than just a nine-to-five job. Actors had to also be promoters, they had to go out front and meet the people—or the odds were they wouldn't be working actors for too long.

When Pat Weaver had long ago told his daughter that show business was a tough racket and that he didn't know if she could handle it, he probably wasn't merely talking about the long hours of work, but how much of her private life she would have to give up. In the long run it is far easier for actors from a poor background to understand just how important the public perception of them really is. Like Sigourney, those from a privileged background have just never lived through the daily struggle to know or have any basis for an understanding. Through characters like Lauren, and through working with directors like Swaim, she was beginning to find out how many women lived. For the strong-willed actress, Lauren was a challenge. Still, she could see just how hard Swaim had fought to be able to direct the film, and this passion made her work just as hard as well.

With her costar, Michael Caine, she found herself shooting with someone who was much different from herself in both background and acting style. *Half Moon Street* was just one of nine films he was making in 1985. While she had spent hours researching China and its history because her character was a student of that subject and she wanted to react and be motivated like Lauren, Caine didn't bother wondering about much of anything aside from his lines and when and where he was supposed to deliver them. Sigourney, the very serious actor, had never seen anyone like him. Ironically, rather than putting her off, he impressed her.

"I think his whole perspective of the business is so refreshing. He works very hard, but then he says, 'I'm going to do this in one take so I can get home to dinner and see my wife.' And he comes on the set with that attitude; it's very professional. He never holds himself back from anyone, and he also has a great deal of taste, which we needed in this movie because of the sex. He just has so much experience that he just does it all intuitively, whereas I really sit down and break down a script and figure it out . . . I still approach it as theater.

"Michael works, but I don't know how he works. I really have no idea."

Sigourney walked away with respect, and possibly a little more knowledge that there are many different methods in acting. Then again, being married to a director may have already begun to open that door of understanding for her. Whatever it was, the superb actress seemed to be maturing greatly as a person.

The movie was not widely reviewed in the

United States, and really didn't find an audience at all until it was released in video. *USA Today,* which had usually been kind to Sigourney and her films, took a look at it and gave it the lowest rating possible: one star. In his review, Mike Clark would call the film "Half-baked." Janet Maslin of *The New York Times* was even less kind. The last line of the review read, "If this film asks anything at all, it's how someone this smart can turn out to be dumb." The line was unfortunately intended for Sigourney's benefit.

From *Half Moon Street,* Sigourney moved on without stopping to her second film of the year, *One Woman or Two.* Once again she would be working on a film outside the Hollywood sphere of influence. The Daniel Vigne film also featured Gerard Depardieu, Michel Aumont, and famous talk-show hostess Dr. Ruth Westheimer and was made on location in France.

The film, a unique experience for an American actor, was shot with the various players speaking their native languages. Subtitles were added later. Added to this unique and somewhat confusing feature was that it was a rapidly paced comedy with timing made for laughs. Amazingly enough, it worked.

One Woman or Two's plot is complicated and difficult to explain. Basically, Sigourney's character (Jessica Fitzgerald) is a fashion model from New York who is mistaken for a female head of a foundation from America interested in meeting with a man who has discovered the fossilized remains of the first Frenchwoman. Ironically, the woman Sigourney impersonates is played by Dr. Ruth, who is about a foot shorter and many years older! From there, this case of mistaken identities gets wilder and wilder with love blooming and the country of France finding out that their first female was black. If the movie had been made in Hollywood in the forties, Cary Grant would have probably been teamed with Irene Dunne. To say the least, it was screwball.

Still, the film would not become an American hit. It has always been difficult for any movie with subtitles to be successful in the States, compounded here by a multilanguage format. In Europe it would be widely viewed, and a great number of critics would hail Sigourney as a tremendous comic actress.

For Sigourney the experience of Paris was not a romantic one. She loved the city and the people who worked with her on the film, but her husband had returned to the States to work on two different projects. In New York and then London, she had gotten used to having John around. She missed their conversations and his company very much. Still, the independent actress did manage to learn her way around Paris as well as make a number of new friends. The French crew thought she was fantastic, and she enjoyed working with her costar, Gerard Depardieu.

"He was great. We had a wonderful time together. He is a sort of lion of an actor, and he is also very French."

Much like Bill Murray, the Frenchman had a certain kinship with the crew, which is rare in films. He joked, entertained, and poked fun at them. He kept everyone in stitches, and Sigourney found herself constantly amused by his antics. He was the first real joker she had worked with since *Ghostbusters,* and it made the days go by much faster.

"Gerard is always going to be a child. He did this wicked thing to me because we were leaping off these mountains and things, for a shot, and after a while I was quite dazed and felt a little dizzy. Before the take he built a little platform under my foot with dirt so that I wouldn't be afraid of slipping, because you'd slip forever. And he built this sort of platform, being terribly nice to me because I was feeling dizzy and I was having vertigo, and then as soon as I said it was all right and I said, 'Thank you, Gerard,' and we were just talking, he would start to pull away at the little platform so that I started to slip down the hill. He's certainly the most mischievous actor I've ever worked with, which I adore because I like that. We had a good time. I'd love to work with him again on something that didn't have as many comic requirements."

While the filming was fun, the real joy of the film for Sigourney was her part. Once again she was playing a character she liked.

"I play a sophisticated woman, and she is sort of vain and selfish. I really enjoyed playing her."

Still, for her, the movie seemed out of sync and stiff. It was fun, but when it was over she didn't really have any idea if it was any good.

"There are certain big risks that the director takes, some which work and some of which don't. The style is very sort of . . . I've done a lot of comedy; most of it sort of high energy, and this was kind of very lifted, to me, it felt .

unnatural. I think Gerard and I both had problems with the style sometimes, but we ended up having a good time and I made a lot of good friends."

At one time, the mere fact that everything didn't feel right or that the director was screwing up would have probably bothered Sigourney a great deal. But now, she accepted it and looked forward to it being over. She wanted to get back to London. Waiting for her there was a husband, and a role she had thought long dead. Both needed her badly.

15

Sigourney returned to London in mid-1985 to begin work on a "Monster Hit." At the time this was a hope, not a reality, but the movie *Aliens*, a followup to her first film some six years before, would give her a chance to become one of the world's best-known actresses. The initial question for James Cameron, now heading up the project for 20th Century Fox, was: Would Sigourney reprise the role of Ripley? It was a question that even she couldn't answer right off the bat, but she knew that she had always yearned for Ripley.

"I wasn't attracted to the idea of doing a sequel, much. I was skeptical of all the reasons why, and I thought the first one held up very well. But I missed the character. I kept thinking that the reception that a character like Ripley had, the way the audience has really sort of cheered for her, I thought that would spawn more roles like that for women. In fact, I don't really think it has."

It was obvious that while Sigourney wanted a strong role to play, one much like Ripley, the mere idea of doing it simply as another film role would never be a sufficient reason to convince her to do it. She was going to require a good script, with a special emphasis on her character. While she missed Ripley, she also wanted her to return with respect and depth—or not at all.

"Jim Cameron gave me the script. He and our producer, Gail Hurd, had very smart reasons for wanting to do a sequel. They wanted to do their own movie, using some of the elements from the first one, including, particularly, the character of Ripley. So they had the same desire to do something; 'If we're going to do it again, let's do something completely.' They had the same feelings I did, of not wanting to cash in on the success of the first picture. So, really it was the script and the openness of Jim Cameron. He said he would not make the picture without me, and I believed him, because the whole script that he wrote was based on Ripley. That's kind of rare in this business, to come across someone who says you're it, and I was egotistical enough to be moved by that."

All ego aside, Sigourney was not the kind of person who was going to fall strictly for flattery. She was nothing if not true to herself. Many of the choices she had made in her career had been wrong and many had ended in failure, but they had all been based on some need or desire that she felt or wanted to do for what she saw as the best role for her own image of herself as well as her talents.

This part would pay her a million dollars, but money had never been a motivating factor in her decision-making process and it wasn't this time either. Many actresses had taken parts that were beneath them, pulled off clothes to do nude scenes simply because they needed the money, but Sigourney had never been hungry enough to be put under the gun to do a film. She was driven by growth, both personal and professional. She took the part because playing Ripley was a challenge.

"I could see that it would take me into a whole new realm for the character. And also there were huge changes in terms of her circumstances; it meant I would not play the eager young innocent again. It's not at all like that; it's the same woman, in a sense years later. So that appealed to me."

After having made two films during the first half of the year, jumping directly into a new one was even more of a demand on the actress. For starters she was tired. And now not only was she making another film, but she was the central character, someone who would be involved in almost every minute of the picture.

Unlike the love story and then the comedy she had just completed, *Aliens* was an action film. It would require her to move constantly, be heroic constantly, and physically be put through the paces like no other role in her life. Before making the film she should have had three or four months off to strengthen herself and prepare. But that was impossible.

At the beginning of the movie, Ripley is seen to be a tired and defeated person. She is literally burned out. The mere fact that

Sigourney had to be feeling the same way couldn't help but make her portrayal that much more realistic. But within days after filming began on a set constructed in an old power plant in London, the actress began to get her energy back. As her character's drive grew, so did her own.

"I must say I was up for it when it started; I really thought I would be tired or something, but I wasn't. I was sort of revved up. Once I got to the third one [day of shooting], I was like in high gear."

She was the star in this film, too. The other actors were looking to her for direction and guidance. She was their leader, and for the first time in her film career she began to receive the treatment and respect that had normally been reserved for her costars.

"I was the veteran, and I really enjoyed being the one person who was there every day. It made me happy to be a constant for the other actors. They'd go off, they'd go to Paris, they'd do this, they'd come back—I'd still be there. And I must say I wasn't envious of them . . . I really enjoyed going into work every day."

Sigourney had once again developed a passion for her part like she hadn't developed in years. She constantly went over her script, marking and remarking anything that she felt she needed to be emphasized in some special way. She also discussed the smallest of details of her part with all of those responsible for bringing Ripley to life. If she found something she didn't feel was consistent, she spoke up.

The crew was crazy about her, for she seemed so cognizant of their feelings. Every problem they had became hers, and she always had the time to work out little snags. Once when confronted with having to decide which of three old ladies could play her "daughter" (she was in a time warp) for a snapshot, she found she lacked the toughness to choose. She simply didn't want to hurt any of their feelings, so someone else picked for her.

One of the most satisfying things about replaying Ripley was that Sigourney literally had become her character. Years before she had worried that her parts consumed her too much, that she let them control her life to too great an extent. But in this case, her immersion enabled both cast and crew to play off her much more easily. There were no surprises. She was consistent.

As the days went by, the actress and the crew developed a rapport rarely seen on any type of job. Every person felt that they had become Sigourney's friend, but one person really grabbed the actress's heart and held it, and that was the young lady who played the little girl in the space colony—Carrie Henn.

"She had never worked before, but she was terrific, it was interesting to work with her. She was very instinctive, but also found all of it a little silly sometimes.

"I felt like we were little partners together. She was the only other person in the group, in the movie, who has experienced what I've experienced, who's been up against the alien alone. So, there is a kinship there that sort of transcended age or size or anything else. In a way, I learned from her, and once I found her, I think I took on a lot of her energy. She gave me a reason to fight harder, instead of just surviving. She really inspired me, and she did inspire me, too, as a friend."

In many ways *Aliens* is a better movie than *Alien*. Its characters were more completely formed, the action was a bit more organized, and the special effects were much more elaborate. It wasn't a tale about a haunted house set in outer space; it was a film about war, about love, about motherhood, and about survival. Even the monsters had a reason for what they did, and though we couldn't root for them, we could understand them.

In the original, we cared about the principal characters because they were human. In the sequel, this humanity was exposed in ways that showed greed, compassion, both mistrust and trust, prejudice, and love. We had felt what they felt, we had been as stupid as they had been, we had known people as bad as the bad guys, and we hoped that we could be as courageous as the good guys.

It was a film in which people fell apart, and then were given a chance to redeem themselves. Most of all, it was a movie held together by Sigourney Weaver from beginning to end. She truly was the star.

"The first film has so much majesty to it, it was so beautiful; it had a kind of grace and scope to it that I thought was quite extraordinary. I don't think that this film has that. Jim Cameron said if the first film was the funhouse, then this is the rollercoaster. And that's exactly true. The other one might be more beautiful, but this one is more fun.

"It is more people to root for and against.

I'm sure it works even if you haven't seen the first one, but if you have seen the first one, no one else but Ripley and the audience have seen the first one, so it's one of those things where it's fun to go to the movie and know something that the rest of the cast doesn't know, and they're just waiting for all hell to break loose."

If the story had a negative, it was the violence. Sigourney, a very strong anti-gun person, had a tough time coming to grips with even blowing pretend monsters away with high-powered pretend guns. Still, the transformation of Ripley from an independent loner to an instinctive mother-figure convinced her that she would fight with whatever means possible to save herself and the little girl. The struggle was epic movie-making.

After the shoot was completed and she had left London for New York, Sigourney couldn't stop talking about the movie. More than at any other time in her career, she was going out of her way to tell people how good the film was, to have it be a huge success. And more than at any other time, she seemed to want to push a project, to go beyond acting out the role and returning home, to make sure her role and her film were noticed.

Certainly the interviews helped. But what also helped was the tremendous exposure that both the actress and the film received from the media. Literally thousands of feet of copy were written before the movie had even been released. Then, upon release, the reviews were unbelievable.

Dan Fainaru of the *Jerusalem Post* magazine alerted his country with these stirring words about Sigourney's performance: "She tackles her part with the instincts of a lioness fighting for her cubs. With her imposing stature and rich palette of expressions she should qualify for the major leagues."

USA Today headlined its review of the film with, "Sigourney's got a monster of a hit!" The national paper gave the film its highest rating.

Rolling Stone said that, "Sigourney gives this programmed movie rawness and life."

Time went one better than most of the others. Not only did they call *Aliens* "The Summer's Scariest Movie," but they also put that heading and a lovely photo of Sigourney on their July 28, 1986 cover. The inside article went on to say that *Aliens* was "a sequel that exceeds its predecessor in the reach of its appeal while giving Weaver new emotional dimensions to explore."

Ultimately, the summer's big hit was the film Sigourney had put so much energy and life into making. It was *her* movie, and the others who had been a part of it were relegated to the back seat. She was the star. Somehow, it seemed a bit strange that two movies about sixteen-foot insectlike monsters could have placed her on the cover of one of the world's most prestigious news magazines. It also seemed ironic that a child from the cultured world of New York, raised on the classics and theater, schooled in the finest private schools, educated at Stanford and Yale, and who seemed determined as an actress to find the ultimate strong-woman-of-the-eighties role and not be typecast, could now be almost lionized and marked for superstardom for acting in a pair of monster flicks. Certainly Ingrid Bergman and Meryl Streep were not catapulted into stardom in this manner.

But *Alien* and *Aliens* had served to awaken not only the press and the public to Sigourney, but to also awaken her to the fact that acting was more than preparing your part and reading your lines. It was a business about people, and it wasn't done as much for those who had the parts as for those who watched them.

She now had come full circle and discovered that she could be commercial while remaining true to her art. She also had awakened to the responsibilities and obligations that went with success in her chosen profession. The combination of circumstances that brought her there—experience, both good and bad; a lack of the kind of roles she wanted to play; and hard work—had been brought together and focused through the love of and communication with her husband.

The press and the critics had pretty much overlooked John Simpson, and he had not demanded any recognition at all. Yet ever since he had come into Sigourney's life, her choices of roles and the direction of her work had proven to be much wiser. She also had a much better understanding of the feelings and goals of her costars and directors.

She returned with John to New York, a conquering hero, alive with a feeling of accomplishment and soon to be honored by her peers, the press, and the public. But her main goal now was to work with the man she loved and return to the theater. After three films in eleven months, after almost a year away from the Broadway scene, she was ready to spend some time at home.

16

After their arrival in New York, Sigourney and Simpson relived an old tradition. They packed their bags and headed for the country. Once again they gave of their talents in the summer theater in Williamstown. This time the play was Tennessee Williams's *Summer and Smoke.*

When they returned to the city they began to work on a play that would hopefully bring out the best in both of them. They chose Shakespeare's *The Merchant of Venice.* Sigourney had a strong desire to prove herself in a classical production ever since she had been forced to leave the troubled production of *Macbeth* three years before. The fact that she hadn't been able to complete a project she had started bothered the actress. It made her feel a bit incomplete as a professional.

The play they had chosen to perform was controversial. For starters, many people felt that *The Merchant of Venice* was anti-Semitic, something Sigourney didn't believe. She seemed to think it was about businessmen who conducted their lives and work in a different manner than most people, and that the racial difference was simply a part of the story, especially in view of the historical context.

Still, upon announcing that they were going to bring the play to the stage, the main battle the husband/wife team seemed to be facing was that it appeared as if they were slapping the Jewish people in the face with the production. Wherever Sigourney goes, a little bit of unique passion seems to find its way into her life, and this time it certainly wasn't asked for or expected.

What the play said or didn't say was not the main issue for Sigourney. She was much more concerned about getting back on the stage and being "nourished" by acting the same part, saying the same lines, all with the same people every day. She thought it would help her decide where, and in which direction, she wanted to go next.

This was not Broadway—hardly even close. The play was to be performed at the CSC Repertory on Manhattan's Lower East Side. Sigourney was playing Portia, and opposite her was John Seitz as Shylock. The mere fact that she saw Portia as a modern woman, bright, independent, and honest, made her all the more ready to tackle the challenge of the part. She openly admitted that she felt as though she and Portia had a great deal in common. Yet this view was not universal in scope.

The reviews were not overly kind. In fact, some were downright nasty. The *New York Post* said boldly in its headlines: "Let not the Bard's quality be strained, but lo it has!" The *Daily News* critic headed his review: "No Sale . . . Merchant Lovers Should Shop Elsewhere." But *USA Today* liked the play and Sigourney, so it wasn't a total loss where the critics were concerned. Certainly the opening night party at the trendy Tunnel disco was a huge success. At least it gave the gossip columnists some material for the next-day papers.

When the play closed in mid-January of 1987, not very many people mourned its passing. Nevertheless, Sigourney had loved the experience, and she felt that the cast and crew had come together wonderfully. Furthermore, she had reaffirmed her love of the theater.

Meanwhile, bad reviews of an off-off-Broadway Shakespeare play hadn't really hurt the actress or her career. The Academy of Motion Picture Arts and Sciences had just announced that she had been one of the five actresses chosen for the best actress category for her starring role in *Aliens*. The fact that the role of Ripley had been in a terror or science fiction movie made the nomination that much more rare, and seemed to indicate the esteem in which the Academy regarded her work. Usually, the five spots would have been filled by five actresses from very serious or traditional entertainment films. In this case the other four who received the honor were: Jane Fonda for playing an alcoholic actress in *The Morning After;* Sissy Spacek as an eccentric murderess in *Crimes of the Heart;* Kathleen Turner in the funny and

charming *Peggy Sue Got Married;* and in-
genue Marlee Matlin, a deaf actress, for her
part in *Children of a Lesser God* (opposite
Sigourney's former co-star, William Hurt).
Matlin eventually won the Oscar, but the honor
for Sigourney would not be soon forgotten.

Movie producer Arnold Glimcher contacted Sigourney on the very day her Oscar
nomination was announced. He offered her
a chance to play the lead in the life story of
primate researcher Dian Fossey, who had been
murdered in Rwanda in 1985 under myste-
rious circumstances. One of the most out-
spoken authorities on gorillas in the wild,
controversial and independent Fossey had
been very much like Sigourney herself.

Thanks to the tremendous publicity Fossey
had received through *National Geographic* and
television specials, Sigourney was familiar with
the story. Still, Sigourney was not particularly enamored with animals, and she had
never been around any type of wild creatures. Although Sigourney may have been
thought of as too "New York" for such a role,
those in charge of production had seen something in *Aliens* that reminded them of the
tough, headstrong Fossey. Ripley wasn't afraid

to confront her fears of anything or anybody, and when she had to she got down in the trenches to do the job. *Aliens* signaled a new-found respect for Sigourney and her talent; she was, clearly, much more suited to portray Fossey than either Brooke Shields or Elizabeth Taylor, the two actresses Fossey would have liked to have seen portraying her at different ages. Imagining either of them chatting with gorillas seemed a bit mind-boggling.

For Sigourney the chance to do the "Adventure of Dian Fossey," (the movie hadn't been named at the time) was an opportunity of a lifetime. She loved causes—most of her life had been involved in supporting or protesting against some type of political or social system. Yet she had often been cast in roles that didn't stand for much of anything. Fossey was a real-life fighter, and Sigourney threw herself into the project with her customary dedication.

One of the first things Sigourney did was read everything she could find on Fossey, to help illuminate why a privileged woman from Kentucky would give up a cushy life to travel halfway across the world and live in the most primitive of conditions just to work with wild mountain gorillas. Sigourney continued her research, she became more and more fascinated by Fossey's motivation and drive.

For the very first time, Sigourney was playing a film role about a person who had really lived, and this provided a challenge to "get inside" the very essence of the woman. She couldn't create a hero, as she had with Ripley in the *Alien* movies, and she wouldn't be satisfied unless everyone who knew Fossey saw her reflected in every one of Sigourney's moves and gestures. Literally tens of thousands of feet of film on the researcher was made available for the actress to study, and Sigourney spent hours watching not only the woman with the gorillas, but concentrating on how Fossey talked, moved, and reacted.

Sigourney's effort to study gorillas firsthand in the United States was difficult. An ape in the zoo is a totally different animal from one living in the wild. For everyone involved in the film, learning about mountain gorillas would be done on the job.

Director Michael Apted lectured his star long and hard about the difficulties every member of the cast and crew would face in Africa. There would be no modern facilities, no cafeteria or catered food, no motel rooms, no limos, and no crew of production assistants granting the star's every whim. Unlike a back-lot *Tarzan*, this would be a jungle epic, shot in the jungle, in extreme heat and freezing nights, endless rain, at high altitudes, and with a base camp made up of tents, cots, and rations.

The books, magazine articles, and videotapes Sigourney studied had given her as much information on her character as she could absorb in three months, but none of these had prepared her body for the torture of the African rain forest. In order to get ready for the grueling daily climb up the mountain in Rwanda, she went to Hawaii and trained by running in the hills there. By the time the first of April arrived, she was ready to board a plane to Africa to meet her co-stars face to face.

Her English director was waiting for her. A lawyer who had been educated at Cambridge University, Michael Apted had begun his career as a researcher for Granada Television. He had made the transition from television to movies; his first American film, *Coal Miner's Daughter*, had won him a great deal of acclaim. It had also established his ability to bring the story of real people to the screen in a form both entertaining and true to character. It was no accident that Dian Fossey, from Kentucky like *Coal Miner's* Loretta Lynn, fascinated the director. He felt that Sigourney was just as right for this part as Sissy Spacek had been for Loretta.

Arnold Glimcher, one of the producers, had worked with Debra Winger and Robert Redford in *Legal Eagles* and had spent years clearing all kinds of red tape and government regulations to make the Fossey story. Everything needed to be as realistic as possible, no matter how difficult. An idealist in every sense of the word, he was fascinated by what this film could do for the issue of animal awareness. "I am not interested in films as business ventures; I have to be passionate about them." He believed that Sigourney was the one actress who could deliver the passion and dedication this role needed. And Anna Hamilton Phelan, who had written the highly successful *Mask*, was chosen to adapt the screenplay of *Gorillas in the Mist* from Fossey's own autobiography.

The rest of the crew, most waiting for Sigourney when she arrived, were just as anxious to bring this ambitious story to life. Fossey's life and passion had become their own, and this project had become more than just a job—it was a mission.

For Sigourney (and for most everyone), the jungle was a shock. The accommodations were tents, and each cot was set with its four legs in bowls of water to keep ants from getting into the bed. There were no phones, no real roads, no shops or restaurants, and no television. The rain forest of Rwanda was much as it had been for centuries.

The mountains where the gorillas live are at extremely high altitudes; temperatures vary tremendously and the rainfall is constant. And the only way to get to the gorillas is to walk up through the jungle. The government had given permission for only six people to shoot with the apes each day, so crews were trimmed to the bare minimum. Everyone had to carry much of his or her own equipment up to the site in search of gorillas each day. This meant hours of hard work before any real shooting could begin. It was a logistical nightmare.

Everyone must have wondered what they had signed up for as they fought the elements and the primitive conditions, and especially Sigourney, who appreared in nearly every scene. But it was worth it to be at Karisoke, where Fossey had lived, to see the gorillas in the wild and get to know them, and to meet many of Dian's closest friends.

Life magazine asked Sigourney to record her thoughts and experiences in a diary-type article for publication to coincide with the film's release. The normally publicity-shy Sigourney, given the creative freedom to write the piece her way, agreed. It would become a moving tribute to Fossey and the entire project.

Alphonse, a native tracker, was assigned to Sigourney to help her negotiate the jungle underbrush, and taught her how to make the proper gorilla vocalizations and body gestures. This would prove very useful—not only for filming, but for survival in the Virunga Mountains.

Shooting began on June 1, 1987, and for six weeks the principal crew worked with Sigourney with the gorillas. Improvisation would be necessary. The filming that was done—and what could be used of it—would depend solely on how well the animals accepted the actress and interacted with her.

On the first day, as soon as the crew made the hike up the mountain and set up near the gorillas, Sigourney was approached by a female. The ape appeared friendly, and the actress responded in a similar manner. As the cameras rolled a protective male leader appeared from the bush and moved quickly and threateningly toward Sigourney. This was how she described it: "I quickly went into the submissive position Alphonse had taught me and hoped for the best. When you have four hundred pounds of pissed-off gorilla inching up on you, you start seeing your life flash by."

Luckily, the gorilla soon realized Sigourney was harmless, and the gorilla groups began to accept her as they had Fossey. Throughout the shoot, Sigourney looked forward to her daily visits in the jungle. Leaving it all behind hurt her deeply. It was like no wrap party she had every had.

The crew was awed by the accomplishments of the actress both on film and with the apes. None of them could say enough about what she brought to the role.

"She is the bravest actress I have every known," said Glimcher. "I can't think of anyone else who could have done it. The first day she went out to the gorillas they came over to her, touched her, and accepted her."

SIGOURNEY WEAVER • 217

Michael Apted added, "Sigourney Weaver was born to play this role. She fell into it so naturally; her physical strength, her attitude, her looks. It's all those things and more."

Perhaps the highest compliment came from Roz Carr, another American woman who was Fossey's closest friend in Rwanda. After viewing the film, she couldn't get over what Sigourney had brought to it. "Sigourney Weaver is perfect as Dian, and I'm so grateful for that," she said. "She's really made herself into a second Dian. It's quite remarkable."

The first word that came to mind about Fossey was dedication, and the first word that came to mind after viewing Sigourney's effort on this film was also dedication. When filming concluded Sigourney said, "I don't believe that any movie *has* to be made, but I really wanted to make this movie. It will send out Dian's beliefs, her passion to more people. Most people love animals; it's a short step to loving the more exotic animals and realizing they're equal citizens of the earth with us. Dian Fossey has changed the future for mountain gorillas through her work, and I'm really glad we're able to tell her story."

With the role over, Sigourney could easily have forgotten the movie and Fossey and returned to her habitual lifestyle in the big city. But she didn't. She set to work in a very un-Sigourney-like manner, spending many weeks on the road publicizing the picture and Fossey's work. Everywhere the public turned, Sigourney was there.

She announced that she was starting a program to adopt gorillas in the wild. she was so filled with passion for this venture and the plight of her animal friends that she tried to get many of her well-to-do associates to join her. For all her close friends—those who had watched her pass through stage after stage and fad after fad—this new whim appeared to be no passing fancy. The woman who had never really embraced a close relationship with a pet now couldn't do enough for animals.

She named her new adopt-a-mountain-gorilla program "Digit," after Fossey's favorite gorilla who'd been murdered by poachers. She promised that all who joined her in this mission would receive updates, photographs, and would know the gorilla they sponsored on a first-name basis. Whether the program does or doesn't work, it will no doubt help the gorilla's cause by creating a new public awareness of their continued plight. Meanwhile, as Sigourney talked about the gorillas the critics talked about her portrayal of Fossey. Reviews heralded Ms. Weaver's performance as the best of her career:

"Sigourney Weaver gives a wonderfully convincing and powerful performance," stated Joel Siegel of *Good Morning, America.*

"A major credit for this [film's success] must go to Sigourney Weaver, whose indomitable presence brings the ghost of Fossey to life for the viewer. It's a sterling performance and one that shows her true range of talent," wrote Carl Hoover for the Cox News Service.

Richard Schickel of *Time* didn't care much for the film, but he gave high marks to the actress, claiming that her performance was "strong and stark."

Review after review echoed the sentiment that this was the role of her life—a part that would position her at the top with a handful of other talented actresses, including Meryl Streep. Hopefully, many more challenging roles will come her way, the same type of plum parts that Katherine Hepburn had claimed as her own during her brilliant career. With Sigourney, the movie business has an actress who can do it all. Her next release, *Working Girl*, starring Harrison Ford and Melanie Griffith, teamed her with hit director Mike Nichols. After the rigors of jungle shoot-

ing, this comedy provided the perfect anti-
dote to roughing it in the wild.

Much more than ever before, the future
appears to be squarely in Sigourney's own
hands. With Jerry Weintraub, she has formed
a production company called Goat Kay Productions, and they're looking for suitable
properties to film. Weintraub has vowed that
all their films will have no more than a PG-
13 rating and will be very commercial. Con-
versely, Sigourney has claimed that she wants
to bring some of playwright Yukio Mishima's
works to the screen, and she wouldn't mind
taking a risk with scripts that would mean
fighting the ratings board tooth and nail. The
end results of this collaboration could be ex-
ceedingly interesting, and hopefully will show
the full range of talent and good judgment of
these two strong-willed people.

And while nothing that Sigourney does is
ever predictable, there is one thing that can
now be stated with some degree of certainty.
She will never again have to beg for a role.

"If someone goes, 'She's too tall,' I go, 'Fine!'
I just don't campaign for parts. I used to campaign; I used to fly across the ocean to meet
people so I could convince them I was right
for this or that. Life is too short and there are

too many other wonderful people to work with. And also, you often don't get those things, the things that you just dream of getting are usually the things that you realize you could have done without. The things that you never suspected would give you as much value back are the things that do."

The Sigourney of old had dreams of changing the world with her acting. She wanted to prove that she was the best, and that she could handle any kind of role. She dreamed big, but now the dreams seem to be scaled down to a more realistic level. But one thing hasn't changed, not since childhood—how she wanted to expand as a person, to grow into something she hadn't been before. Her future may not be in acting—with her determination and talent, she could tackle anything.

"I think most actors would say that they'd like to have more to do with the projects that they're working on. And so I have a lot of ideas for a number of films, some of which have nothing to do with my being in them. I'm working on a script with my friend Chris Durang for [director Ivan] Reitman if he still wants it. Then I have a couple of projects that I'm talking to people about."

For Sigourney, the million dollars she re-

222 • SIGOURNEY WEAVER

ceived for *Aliens* and *Gorillas in the Mist* brought no more satisfaction than the $311.75 she received for summer stock. She judges herself through her work, not her paycheck. She has been—and she knows it—a lucky lady.

By the same token, the security that she feels about herself, having been raised to walk to a different beat as well as not worrying about critics or having her face on the cover of every magazine, will also keep her from ending up like the Marilyn Monroes of the world, a tragedy of overindulgence. She feels comfortable with what and who she is.

This knowledge of herself, coupled with her strong desire to be heard and under- stood, will probably also give her marriage a better chance of survival in the fickle world of show business, because both she and her husband are somehow not a part of that strange world even when they are working in it.

While nothing is a sure bet when dealing with a person who is as unconventional as Sigourney Weaver, it is almost certain that she will hold on to the things she knows are important while expanding into areas she feels could use her talents. Just like her father, she will continue to look for the open doors of opportunity and imagination.

One role she has repeatedly claimed that she wants to try is that of being a mother. At thirty-eight, time is running out for her chances at being picked for this challenging part. There is much suspicion that the reason she isn't actively pushing for a new and exciting role in a film is that she is concentrating on trying to bring motherhood into her life. Certainly, her portrayal as Ripley in *Aliens* would lead the casual onlooker to believe that she possesses the necessary instincts to do a great job with kids. And while she talks about children a great deal, she also says that her kids will not stop her work. So what does the future hold?

"I feel that there is something very specific I'm here to do that I haven't done yet." Beyond that, even Sigourney hasn't begun to pin down what it is. What she believes is that the best of her is yet to come. Hopefully we will all benefit if that work is on film. No doubt, no matter where or what it is, she will benefit, too.

FILMOGRAPHY

ALIEN
(1979)
Costars: Tom Skerritt
                                  Yaphet Kotto
                                  William Hurt
Director: Ridley Scott

EYEWITNESS
(1981)
Costars: William Hurt
                                  Christopher Plummer
                                  James Woods
Director: Peter Yates

YEAR OF LIVING DANGEROUSLY
(1983)
Costars: Mel Gibson
                                  Linda Hunt
                                  Bill Kerr
Director: Peter Weir

DEAL OF THE CENTURY
(1983)
Costars: Chevy Chase
                                  Gregory Hines
Director: William Friedkin

GHOSTBUSTERS
(1984)
Costars: Dan Aykroyd
                  Bill Murray
                  Harold Ramis
Director: Ivan Reitman

HALF MOON STREET
(1986)
Costar: Michael Caine
Director: Bob Swaim

ONE WOMAN OR TWO
(1986)
Costars: Gerard Depardieu
                  Michel Aumont
                  Dr. Ruth Westheimer
Director: Daniel Vigne

ALIENS
(1986)
Costars: Carrie Henn
                  Michael Biehn
                  Paul Reiser
Director: James Cameron